419

Children's Art Education

A NOTE ABOUT THE AUTHORS

This book represents the work of two young women, and the
cooperation of many other persons—students, fellow teachers,
administrators, and special consultants. It is based on
principles of art education long developing and frequently
expressed through individual leaders and national, regional
and state organizations of the field. The manuscript originated in a series of classroom experiences, recorded in
the form of conversations between art teachers and elementary students of Minneapolis. It has grown to its present
status only because the true, dedicated spirit of the artist-
teacher-scholar-writer prevailed, through years of critical
examination and re-examination, and hard, creative revision.

ESTELLE HAGEN KNUDSEN: Consultant in art (with
F. Edward Del Dosso), Minneapolis Public Schools. Planned
the content of the present art guide for the school system,
elementary through high school. Is a sensitive, accomplished
artist in many media. Has B.S. and M.E. degrees in art
education from the University of Minnesota, and did ad-
vanced work at the University of Oslo, Norway. Previous
publications include articles for *School Art* and *Arts and
Activities* magazines.

ETHEL MADILL CHRISTENSEN: Former helping teacher
of art, Minneapolis Public Schools, concurrently with Mrs.
Knudsen. Also has B.S. and M.E. degrees in art education
from the University of Minnesota. Now resides with her
husband in a southern university city but continues her
expanding interest in oil painting, which she has successfully exhibited.

Knudsen & Christensen

Children's Art Education

Chas. A. Bennett Co., Inc.
PEORIA, ILLINOIS

Copyright 1957
ESTELLE HAGEN KNUDSEN and
ETHEL MADILL CHRISTENSEN
All Rights Reserved.
Library of Congress Catalog Card Number: 57-5429
PRINTED IN THE U. S. A.
Second Printing
26VH33

CONTENTS

ACKNOWLEDGMENTS

Many people associated with the Minneapolis Public School System aided and influenced us in the writing of this book. The inquiring classroom teachers originally stimulated us to attempt the project. Dr. F. Edward Del Dosso, art consultant, and the late Bess Foster Mather, former art consultant, willingly read an early draft of the manuscript. Mrs. Angeline P. Spell, consultant in art, also offered many helpful suggestions. Miss Viola Knudson, first grade teacher, and Dr. Sarah Holbrook, senior psychologist, read and criticized parts of the manuscript. Miss Lillian Jasperson, Mr. Thomas Kent, and Mr. George McDonough helped with the photographs of the school rooms and children at work. A special acknowledgment is due the children who so graciously let us illustrate the manuscript with their work.

Dr. Clifford M. Christensen, University of Arkansas, and Dr. Kalmer E. Stordahl, Washington, D. C., were helpful in evaluating relevant research and in the clarification of the concepts in Part One.

We are also grateful to our husbands, Howard and Clifford, for their patience and moral support.

All these individuals, and many more, deserve credit and we are most appreciative of their help. We, of course, retain full responsibility for any faults in the book.

INTRODUCTION

This book is based on our experiences with the art program in the Minneapolis Public Schools. We worked with over a thousand elementary teachers ranging from kindergarten through grade six, in 75 elementary schools throughout the city.

We began by organizing the elementary art program around three main services. (1) The first of these services was demonstration teaching. The teachers requested the particular art lessons they wished to see taught, via the school principal, or sometimes directly from us. Usually we presented from three to four demonstrations each day. While most of the teacher requests were for classroom demonstrations, some preferred a conference. Due to the large number of teachers, however, individual assistance was limited to approximately two or three visits per school during the year. (2) To supplement this program, after-school, in-service courses were organized for the teachers who felt that they would like more help. However, these two services did not answer all the teachers' needs. They wanted to know more about how to teach, how to arrange attractive displays of children's work, and how to handle each art medium. (3) Therefore it became necessary to add a third service: a set of bulletins on the various art media. Because adequate material of this nature was not available, we decided to assemble our own. Noticing the frequency with which certain questions were asked, we built bulletins on these questions. They proved to be an efficient way of relating information to the teachers.

7

This book is the product of our experiences in the setting just described. It was motivated by a real need among the elementary school teachers. Favorable reactions to the material in the book have been obtained from elementary teachers. It has been very helpful to those with little or no art training. We feel that the same principles and techniques would be useful to parents, camp leaders, settlement house workers, and anyone else interested in guiding the creative activities of children.

We have made no attempt to survey all art education research and theories. The purpose of our book has been to describe the art education methods that we used in the Minneapolis elementary schools. The children's illustrations in this book are the results of these methods.

Our writing approach has been to start with a necessary assumption, build a *frame of reference* to guide the teacher, and explain it by presenting *actual examples of classroom teaching*. Deliberately, we have given little consideration to the controversial issues in art education because we doubt that effective art teaching methods will be discovered via debate. As in the sciences, the answers must come from properly conducted research. One need not look far to discover the meager research in elementary art education methods.

Excellent summaries can be found in the following sources:

Goodenough, Florence L. "Studies in the Psychology of Children's Drawings." *Psychological Bulletin,* 25:272-283, 1928.
Goodenough, Florence L., and Harris, Dale B. "Studies in the Psychology of Children's Drawings: II, 1928-1949." *Psychological Bulletin,* 47:369-433, 1950.
National Society For the Study of Education. *Art in American Life and Education.* Fortieth Year Book, Bloomington, Ill.; Public School Publishing Co., 1941.
Schultz, Harold A., and Roos, Frank J. "Art Education." *Encyclopedia of Educational Research* (W. S. Monroe, ed.) New York: Macmillan Co., pp. 64-72, 1950.

Most of the research has been concerned with developmental

levels, projective techniques, study of the personality, mental testing, the relationship of art ability, and personality variables. Virtually none of the research has been concerned with art education teaching methods.

What is the evidence for the views presented in this book? Primarily, it consists of the art products of the children who were taught by the methods we describe. These methods grade school teachers can understand and use. The evidence may seem far from ideal, but it is in fact highly reliable.

We have explained various philosophies, theories, and opinions of art to the elementary school teachers. Invariably the same question occurs, "What do these philosophies and theories suggest that we do in the classroom?" We could not successfully answer this question, not because theorizing or philosophizing is a useless activity, but because the present theories and philosophies do not seem to be grounded in actual experiences or observable events. Many popular authorities on art education maintain only indirect contact with child activities.

In our practices and in this book, we have built a frame of reference to guide the teacher. It is presented in considerable detail to make it understandable. Our beginning assumption is that *children gain something* from effective art expression. In other words, we believe that art is a worth-while activity for the child. At the core of our frame of reference is the belief that expression through an art medium is a form of motivated behavior that can be satisfying and rewarding to the child. This grounds our frame of reference in observable events and suggests the application of facts from the field of psychology.

We have found that elementary teachers and principals find the frame of reference understandable and useful. Many have commented on the similarity between our frame of reference and the ones used in other areas of learning. In our opinion, this type of relationship is healthy and profitable.

The first part of our book consists of a description of our frame of reference and the art process. This is followed by a group of art experiences which illustrate the application of the concepts we consider necessary to guide the children toward growth and satisfaction. In order to give the reader a feeling and understanding for the type of working relationship which must exist between the teacher and the children, these experiences are records of actual classroom situations. Analysis and discussion of the teaching situation follow each chapter.

The next section considers topics which we have found stimulate children effectively. Art media appropriate to the various age groups follow. We include the media we consider the most basic to the elementary school art activities. The information in the media chapters is based on the inquiries of the elementary teachers as we worked with them. The problems include various phases of art experiences with a certain medium. Only the most frequent problems are presented with concrete answers.

Because many classroom teachers ask for assistance in organizing the physical properties of the classroom as well as the display areas, one chapter considers pertinent ideas on this down-to-earth subject.

As a summary of all our beliefs, checklists are the basis of the concluding chapter. The reader can use them as a self-inventory.

We think the reader will profit most from this book if the first part is read in its entirety. Although you may be particularly interested in the second grade children, for example, a study of all the classroom situations will increase your understanding of the basic teaching concepts. In turn, you will be able to work more effectively with second grade children. Early familiarization with the suggested topics and media will also prove helpful. For information about a certain medium, refer to the media chapters as the need arises. A careful consideration of the children's illustrations deepens the general understanding.

FRAME OF REFERENCE & THE ART PROCESS

This section describes the frame of reference which helped to influence our thinking and practices in guiding the art experiences of children.

The term "frame of reference" is what some educators call a philosophy, a point of view, or a theory based on experience. Essentially, it is a rationale underlying the specific techniques and methods of teaching. With the accumulation of evidence in properly conducted research, a particular frame of reference may be modified, accepted as valid, or rejected as invalid in light of the facts collected. If a frame of reference is established as a valid one, then it becomes more than a rationale. It becomes a means of developing the processes under consideration.

Our frame of reference is a rational structure to which the teacher can refer when a problem arises. Of course, it not only provides the teacher with what to do, but it also should give him or her some understanding of the reasons for the methods and techniques. It offers a tentative explanation of the processes involved.

The frame of reference which evolved from our experiences is simple but of considerable utility. However, we do not say that it gives an adequate explanation of all art teaching methods. We hope it will be augmented by experience and research on the teacher's part.

11

THE ART PROCESS

The art process begins with the child who has had experiences and a desire to express ideas and feelings about his experiences, which may include a birthday party or a visit to an airport or to a firehouse. The child verbally expresses ideas and feelings about these experiences to his parents, friends, and teachers. He may also have the opportunity to interpret them through music, prose, or the dance. Pictorial art is only one means of expression. Of course, individuals vary in their ability to express themselves in each medium. One child may express himself adequately in writing but more effectively through an art medium. The opposite may be true of other children. What a child does when expressing his ideas and feelings in a certain medium is a form of behavior. It is important to regard the child's activity as a *behavior* because then careful observation and research is possible. This kind of thinking grounds the art process in observable events. It then becomes less mysterious and more closely related to other child activities and behaviors.

Research lends some support to the notion that a child expresses his inner ideas and feelings through his art activities. In their survey of research, Goodenough and Harris conclude that generally investigators agree that a child draws what he *feels* rather than what he *sees or knows.* "A child in his drawings frequently gives outward expression to his inner life of thoughts and feelings, to his fears and his desires, to his hopes and his frustrations."

Intelligence and Emotion

For clarity, think of the art process as involving two basic elements: the *intellectual* and the *emotional.* These two components are inter-related and probably inseparable.

The intellectual aspect is concerned with the formal elements of the child's expression. These things the child knows or discovers when expressing himself in an art medium. They are the tools and techniques. For example, when a child consciously repeats a color in his design he uses a more intellectual approach to his art problem. Likewise, when a child consciously organizes the center of interest in his picture, he employs the intellectual approach. A child who decides to use a dry-brush technique to paint a tree trunk uses a method that may have been taught him. He expresses himself by what he knows.

The emotional element, on the other hand, may be characterized by spontaneity, feeling, and intuition. Instead of planning his picture, the sensitive child appears to feel its structure. His emotions determine his choice of color and texture. He uses just the right color not by thinking, but by feeling that it is the right color.

A child may also respond emotionally to a particular topic—often indicated by young children who add or subtract elements in their drawings. For instance, the soft-spoken boy who says he left the ears off his dad's picture because he never listened to him anyway. A stubborn little girl, who had been reprimanded for wearing rouge, drew a picture of herself with big red cheeks. A child sometimes exaggerates parts of his picture when he connects it with a strong emotional experience. For instance, after having been firmly held and spanked, a boy drew his father with an unusually large arm. It is exceedingly important to consider this emotional aspect in child art. The child who enters freely into an art activity because he has an inner thought or feeling to communicate produces unique and genuine art.

Desire For Expression

A desire for expression through an art medium is evident with very young children. Though the time that children are willing to devote to their expressions varies with their interest and development, this desire appears to be a basic need. A number of writers in the art field have recognized two things: (1) the children's desire to express themselves, and (2) the effectiveness of art media for expression. Lowenfeld, in particular, speaks of the "deeply rooted creative impulse." He is confident that children would produce creative work without additional stimulation if they were free from interference in their development. Lowenfeld implies that creative expression is an inherent characteristic. But whether it is inherent or something which is learned or at least greatly stimulated by contact with others need not concern us here. It is sufficient to recognize that a strong desire to ex-

13

press oneself exists and that everyone gains satisfaction from effective expression.

Basic Teaching Concepts

Assuming that the expression of thoughts and feelings is important, the question arises, "What classroom conditions are necessary to bring about this expression?"

We think that the understanding and application of six general concepts are necessary for effective children's art education: (1) permissive atmosphere, (2) stimulation, (3) guidance, (4) acceptance, (5) developmental levels, and (6) evaluation. Following is a discussion of each.

Permissive Atmosphere

This is an atmosphere that *condones* the expression of the child's own feelings and ideas. It encourages him to tell about experiences that are personal and unique. In such an atmosphere he is encouraged to express his ideas and feelings in his own way. During the art experience he is given ample opportunity to explore and to experiment with a variety of media. The child then arrives at an individual way of working.

A permissive atmosphere is determined to a large extent by the teacher's attitude, tone of voice, gestures, and verbal approval; in general, the *spirit* of the presentation.

Of course, there are limits within such an atmosphere. The child cannot do anything he wants. The teacher-suggested general topic limits the child to express a personal experience within that topic. He is also asked to use the media provided, which are determined by his developmental level. Though the aim in a permissive atmosphere is to encourage the child to express himself freely, restrictions which apply to other areas of learning also exist with art activities.

Stimulation

The teacher can awaken and motivate children to express their ideas and feelings in many ways.

For effective art expression, suggest topics related to children's immediate interests and experiences. Discussion, demonstration, and sometimes the presentation of an unfamiliar medium stimulate expression.

To arouse the child's thoughts and feelings, a ten to fifteen minute discussion may be necessary. When a topic based on a recent experience of the children is selected, only a few minutes may be needed to stimulate them. The teacher may ask some children to give a detailed description of their experiences. From others, it might be just a brief response. The aim is to motivate as many children as possible. Sometimes children can be stimulated by watching other children pantomime some of their experiences.

Stimulation is anything the teacher does to excite the desire within children to paint, to color, or to model their ideas and feelings about a topic. The type of stimulation depends on the weather, the time of day, the art media, the experiences, the interests, and the developmental levels of the children. The length of the stimulation period varies with all art experiences.

Guidance

The teacher guides the children to express themselves honestly and effectively in order that the art activities will be satisfying to them. This involves (1) helping the children select and clarify their thoughts and feelings and (2) presenting media and techniques at the proper time.

When helping children, the teacher needs to remember that they have had fewer experiences than adults. Experiences of very young children revolve around themselves and their immediate environment. However, as children grow older they establish more relationships with people; consequently their experiences grow in number and variety.

The teacher may help the children clarify their thoughts or feelings by an individualized detailed discussion of the topic. Usually only a few children need this kind of personal guidance. For example, as the second graders were placing their clay pieces on a table to dry, a very upset child said, "I don't know how to make an elephant. I know what it looks like, but I can't make it." As a host of sympathetic classmates surrounded him, the teacher sat down to talk with him about the elephant with his heavy legs and his stocky body. Soon, the boy started to work with more confidence. His idea of an elephant was clearer in his mind.

The teacher also needs to provide the children with media at the appropriate time and to guide them in the necessary procedures, if any. This type of guidance is dependent on the children's developmental level. To illustrate: a six-year-old handles only very simple media and simple techniques as compared to a child of nine. Of course, variations of ability exist within a single grade or age.

Acceptance

A positive attitude toward the children and their works indicates the teacher's acceptance of them. The teacher recognizes that children have interests which differ from adults. Children express child ideas, feelings, and concerns in childlike ways. The teacher is understanding and considerate of their ideas and feelings in whatever form they express them.

Children have levels of development in art as well as other subject areas. The child's particular developmental level is accepted by letting him work in his natural way. Guidance is given in a kindly way. Teacher enthusiasm for differences is revealed continuously.

The teacher demonstrates acceptance by the importance attached to the art work. For example, by attractively displaying the child's art, the teacher gives it prestige and prominence.

Developmental Levels

Knowledge of developmental levels and the procedures involved in handling each medium is necessary to effectively guide the art experiences of children. Many writers, Viktor Lowenfeld in particular, have classified children's drawings into general stages of development. Following is a very brief summary of the developmental stages of child art:

The Scribbling Stage. To adult eyes, some kindergarten children's drawings appear to be only scribbles. However, by talking and by listening to the child's explanations about his picture, it is apparent that sometimes the scribbles represent objects and people, or at least a pleasing use of line and color. Usually these scribbles are linear and are drawn in colors which the child just happens to use. Expressing himself in this way seems to be adequate to the child. There appears to be no question in his mind as to whether or not he has "art" ability.

When manipulating a three dimensional medium, the very young child works in masses. Little detail is included. The child is particularly interested in the feel of the art material. He names his forms "Waffles" or "Candy" or "Airplanes."

As the child becomes older, his scribbles grow in meaning. He begins to use more detail, such as lines to represent legs or arms. Sometimes he emphasizes elements of special significance: For instance, the length of a person's body may be exaggerated or (conversely) the child may omit parts which are unimportant to his idea.

He does not always draw people or things. Sometimes he fills his paper with lines and colored areas to make a "pretty design."

The Symbolic Stage. In the first, second, and third grades, the people and things in the child's drawing become more recognizable. Objects from his environment are often placed on a ground line which is either on or above the edge of the paper. If the ground line is above the edge of the paper, the bottom of the paper is usually green to represent grass. Another characteristic of an outdoor scene is a blue band to represent the sky, which is usually parallel to the top edge of the paper . . . and often a sun is included. By this time, the child relates colors to the object.

Occasionally other, seemingly strange, characteristics appear in the child's drawings during this stage of development. For example, he might simultaneously show parts of both the inside and outside of an object. He might reason that this is better than showing only one aspect of it.

17

Similar changes appear in the child's three-dimensional work. Though basically the forms are symbolic rather than realistic, they become more recognizable and detailed. Often a child makes his forms sit, walk, or run as he portrays them.

The Transition Stage. Sometimes during the grades four, five, or six the child seems to become very self-conscious of his work. As a result, his people become awkward and stiff in appearance. He becomes so conscious of detail that he may want to use a pencil. Perfection and realism are often the ideals. This intense interest in the appearance of the end product forces goals often beyond his reach.

When drawing or painting during this stage of artistic development, the children bring the sky down to meet the horizon. They also begin to show distance by overlapping objects. Sometimes, both the top view and the side view of objects are included in the picture—as if unfolded like a hinged screen.

The subject matter of the child's work even seems to change. More children are vitally interested in specific things such as horses, cars, airplanes, or persons. Also noticeable is some children's preference for certain art media and the desire occasionally to work together on murals, puppet shows, or mobiles.

The children will be at many different levels in the same class. Sometimes, a child regresses temporarily in his developmental sequence. This may happen when he is confronted with a new medium or when he has a severe emotional reaction to the topic or the medium. Whatever the cause, he is worth special attention till he regains poise.

Evaluation

The ideas and feelings the child has attempted to express, his behavior, his growth and development, and his way of handling the art medium may be used to evaluate the child's art experience. It is mainly an activity done by the teacher sometimes alone or at other times during or at the end of the art experience. A short individual evaluation of the child's work during the art experience often helps the child clarify his thoughts and feelings. Evaluation is given only when the child or a group of children is psychologically ready for it.

During the group evaluation of the end products the main emphasis should be on the ideas and feelings that the child has attempted to express. The child's technique of handling media is important only as an aid for him to express himself more effectively.

With primary grade children, there should be little emphasis on techniques. Analysis of techniques confuses them. Even some upper graders are not mature enough to understand and to apply abstract concepts and complicated techniques.

Constructive evaluation helps to increase the child's understanding and enjoyment of his own work as well as his classmates' creations.

PART ONE CLASSROOM ART EXPERIENCES

1. KINDERGARTEN

Topic **"How I help"**

- stimulating expression through a discussion of a common childhood experience

- questioning skillfully to clarify the children's personal experiences

- helping children choose suitable art media

- encouraging dramatic play as an interpretation of the general topic

- observing a range of developmental levels within the group

- understanding and respecting the ideas expressed by others

The children sit comfortably in a semicircular group on the floor. The teacher speaks as the door opens. "Children, this is Miss_____. She is the lady I told you would come to visit and be my special 'substitute' today. Miss_____will do the talking, but I will help you all I can as we go along. Is that all right?"

The children nod.

The art teacher smiles and greets them, "Good morning, boys and girls." Then noticing the expressions on their faces, she adds, "You must be doing something you like."

"We were saying some poems together," responds the classroom teacher.

"Maybe you'll say one for me?"

"All right. Let's do the one we just finished."

The children join the teacher as she repeats:

> Mix a pancake, stir a pancake,
>   Pop it in the pan;
> Fry the pancake, toss the pancake,
>   Catch it if you can.

Christina G. Rossetti, "Sing-Song." *Time for Poetry,* by May Hill Arbuthnot, Scott Foresman, p. 175.

"You certainly said that well, boys and girls. I liked the way you acted it out, too. Do some of you help your mother make pancakes?"

"Sometimes I do."

"I help, too . . . when she lets me."

"*When* do you help?" questions the teacher as she moves to the piano bench vacated by the classroom teacher.

"After supper."

"*What* is it that you do to help your mom, then?"

"I wash the dishes and wipe them all by myself," Sue says **proudly.**

21

"I wash for Mom, too," murmurs Lloyd.

"What do *you* wash?"

"The floor."

"Can you show us *how* you wash the floor?"

> **He crawls on his knees toward the piano as he vigorously swings his arms like a pendulum over the floor.**
> **A few children imitate his movements.**

"My, you certainly need strong arms and legs when you wash the floor." Then she inquires, "How do the rest of you help at home?"

"I help fix my dad's car."

"Where do you usually fix it, Gary?"

"At the gas station."

"What do you see at the gas station?"

"The gas station man."

"And what do you do to help your dad fix the car?"

"I hold the flashlight."

"Gary, would you show us how you hold the flashlight?"

> **As Gary pretends to hold a make-believe flashlight, the teacher directs the children's attention to the position of his hands. They observe that his fingers curve to hold the flashlight securely.**

"Thank you, Gary. Now, let's look at our hands." Together they talk about the parts of their hands. Then all the children show the position of their hands when they help at home.

Others are invited to talk about how they help at home. It is necessary to ask many questions to encourage these children to recall their experiences clearly.

Kathy, who says she helps put her toys away, is asked, "Where do you usually put your toys?"

"In the toy box."

22

"Where do you store your toy box?"

"In the closet."

"What are some of the toys you like very much?"

"Oh, my dolls and lots and lots of blocks."

Eagerly a tall chubby boy bursts forth, "Sometimes I get nails and hammer for my dad."

"What does your dad do with the nails and hammer when you bring them to him?"

"He fixes things for my mom. Once he made a shelf for my room."

"Show me how a nail looks."

With his thumb and index finger, he makes a circle. He uses one finger from his left hand to show the point of the nail, thrust through the circle.

"My, that's a good description!"

It is apparent that the children help at home in many ways. More than half of them have their hands raised to contribute answers—even those who have already responded.

One boy stands as he gives his answer. "I can draw how I like to help."

"I'd like to see you do that. What would you draw with?"

"Crayons."

"Fine! If some of you would like to draw a picture of how you help, crayons and paper are on some of the tables."

About twenty children hurry toward the tables, which are supplied with 9 x 12 inch and 12 x 18 inch manila paper and large transparent bowls of crayons. Generous chunks of non-hardening clay and construction sets are placed on several other tables. The teacher suggests to the remaining children, "Maybe you would like to work at the other tables to show how you help."

Soon, almost all the children start to work in some medium. One

23

child fits parts of a construction set together, while his neighbor pushes and pulls a colorful piece of clay. Others crayon.

"Can I use the playhouse? I'll show you how I help at home."

"Can I, too?" chime in two others.

"Certainly."

They scamper happily toward the playhouse. In one room one boy begins to dust the newly painted furnishings, while the other two set the dining table.

Three children sit quietly near the piano. With a friendly smile, the teacher challenges each one to express himself in some way. "Who do you help the most?" "What do you like to help with at school?" "What is your favorite toy?" Soon, two of the children begin to work, one at the easel and the other with clay. The third child is extraordinarily shy. He does not respond. The teacher encourages him to work in his favorite medium, powder paint.

As the children work, the teacher mingles among them to encourage and accept their ideas. A range of developmental levels is evident. Some children are engrossed with the designs left by their brush as they move it across the paper. Others work in a more recognizable way.

Melanie wears her daddy's discarded shirt to protect her dress. She paints with a sponge. "My, what a pretty girl you're making!" says the teacher.

"She's going to be helping me sweep the floor," Melanie explains. Then, using a brush this time, she paints the girl's eyes.

Jimmy's drawing is a maze of haphazard lines with a sprinkle of circles. "Tell me about your picture, Jimmy." (On a scratch pad, she then writes his explanation.)

"He's walking down the stairs. My dad tells me to go get his shoes and I do. That's the shoes. That's my two brothers."

"To what room do you bring your dad's shoes, Jimmy?"

"The TV room."

"In your picture you told a good story. Now, maybe you would like to tell about another way that you help. This time you can use clay instead of crayons, if you like." She pats him on the shoulder as she moves toward the next child.

How I Help—
James F., age five

25

How I Help—*Debra S., age five*

A delicate child greets her with a smile. She has crayoned red, yellow, and blue areas on her paper. The individual crayon strokes are easily seen. To enclose each patch of color is an irregular shape drawn with a single line.

The teacher says casually, "This is an interesting shape; I'd like to know more about it."

The little girl looks bewildered.

Quickly, the teacher praises her, "I can see you're having fun with your crayon."

The child smiles and begins to draw again. She is in the beginning scribble stage. Her shapes and colors have no meaning yet.

The teacher listens to several other children tell about their pictures for a few minutes. Then they all return to work.

At this point, a child says unhappily, "I don't think I can make it."

Turning toward her, the teacher responds, "What is it that you want to make?"

"My head."

"What shape is your head?"

The girl thinks about this, observing the teacher's head. She makes a decision. "I know! If I had two pieces of clay."

"I believe more clay is in the plastic container."

Cheerfully, she hurries toward the non-hardening clay.

The quick workers have created both a picture and a clay modeling.

The teacher strokes a musical chord to signal the children to gather around the piano. The children look happy as they hold their pictures, clay forms, and constructions. Suddenly, a peaceful quiet settles over the group. It's a sharp contrast to the previous purposeful noise.

"I have written down some of the ways you help, boys and girls." She scans her paper. "Here's one. 'I take the garbage down.' Who helps in that way?" A broad grin on Greg's face provides the answer.

"If you worked with crayon or paint, show us your pictures. Billy, I think the boys and girls will enjoy yours. Would you show it to all of us?"

Standing close to the teacher, Billy explains, "This is me washing the car. This the parking. This the door. This the tree and this is the turkey on top." The children laugh with delight.

"That would be fun to have a surprise turkey on top of the car!

27

How I Help—
*Billy W.,
age five*

Thank you, Billy." Viewing another picture, she says, "It looks as if David likes to help outside. David, will you tell us more about yours?"

"I'm rakin' the grass. This is my house. My mom is inside cleaning."

Then the group discuss the forms made from clay and the construction sets. "This is me helping fold the clothes." . . . "I made myself running to the store." . . . "I clean closets with my mother and sister." . . . "I help my mom wash the clothes."

"My, you certainly help in many ways," the teacher concludes. "Boys and girls, you've told me how you help at home. Now, where else can you help?"

How I Help—
David B.,
age five

How I Help—
Richard M.,
age five

"Right here."

"At school."

"How can you be helpers right now?"

"Pick up."

"Put the clay away."

"Where does the clay belong? Where are the crayons kept? Let's see if we can put everything back."

> The children scurry as they put the materials and supplies in their storage places. Some stack papers, too. The clay forms are smashed and put into the container. Almost all the children help in some way. One comes to the teacher to point at some curliques on his paper. "I can really write, too."

The teacher responds warmly.

Afterwards, they gather around the classroom teacher. She asks them, "What would you like to say to Miss _____?"

> "When are you coming again?"

"Just as soon as I can. You are doing so well that you don't need me. Did you know that? Well, you are! But I'll come again just because I like to see what you are doing. Goodbye now."

PREPARING FOR THE EXPERIENCE

After consulting with the art teacher, the classroom teacher secured an ample supply of art materials—crayons, 9 x 12 and 12 x 18 inch paper, non-hardening clay and linoleum squares. These materials were arranged on the tables so that they were easily accessible to the children. Sheets of 24 x 36 inch paper were tacked on the easels. Paints, brushes, and other needed materials were also placed at the easels for the children to use. Likewise, the construction sets and the playhouse were available.

All of these media were appropriate to the developmental levels of the children. In addition, the materials were attractive and familiar to the children.

Following is a brief discussion of the methods and techniques of teaching used by the art teacher in the kindergarten art activity:

Permissive Atmosphere

The teacher's warm reception of the children's recitation and dramatization of the poem encouraged the children to respond naturally. Therefore they spoke freely and with ease when the teacher asked them, "*When* do you help?" "*What* is it you do to help your mom, then?" "What do you wash?" and "Can you show us *how* you wash the floor?"

In this permissive atmosphere the children found it easy to express a variety of personal experiences. They responded quickly to this opportunity. Gary explained how he helped his dad fix his car, Kathy told about helping to put her toys away, and another boy eagerly reported about getting the nails and hammer for his dad, who made a shelf for his room. Later, during the art activity, the children were encouraged to visually express their ideas in their individual manner, using media and skills natural to their developmental level.

Stimulation

Because of the children's enthusiasm, the teacher broadened the topic of the Rossetti poem to include other home activities. This enabled each child to express a personal experience. Questions progressing from the general to the more specific details stimulated the children to recall their experiences. Demonstrations by individual children and the group created interest and excitement. The boy who said, "I can draw how I like to help," gave the teacher evidence that she had spent sufficient time in stimulating their ideas.

Guidance

As soon as the children were ready to express themselves, they were encouraged to use any of the available materials. When the three children did not choose any of the art materials, the teacher immediately gave them individual help. She carefully checked to see that everyone was at work and enjoying it. Then, as she moved among the group, she gave the children encouragement to express their personal ideas in their own way, using statements such as, "Tell me more about your picture." . . . "My, what a pretty girl you're making!" . . . "I can see that you're having fun with your crayon." At all times, she was careful not to confuse or embarrass a child with her questions and comments.

When a child finished one expression, the teacher suggested that he use another medium to tell how he helped. Some of these children painted a picture and then modeled in clay. The teacher guided a girl to solve her problem by rephrasing the problem in the form of a question: "What shape is your head?"

Acceptance

Immediately upon entering the classroom, the art teacher responded with warmth and understanding toward the children. She noticed their interest and enthusiasm in reciting poems and asked, "Maybe you'll say one for me?" During the art activity, she used other statements such as "I liked the way you acted it out, too." . . . "In your picture you told a good story." . . . and "That would be fun to have a surprise turkey on top of the car!" to show the children that she accepted their ideas and their ways of working.

When she told the delicate girl, "This is an interesting shape; I'd like to know more about it," she sensed the child's bewilderment. Quickly she praised her work and thus reassured her and accepted her level of development.

Developmental Levels

Most five-year-old children are happy, lively, and uninhibited, with a variety of interests. The little boy who burst forth to tell that he brought his dad the nails and hammer revealed the enthusiasms of this age.

Their interests are centered around their home and their immediate environment. Helping Mom with the dishes, putting away the toys, bringing Dad his shoes, and helping to wash the car are all important experiences to these children.

The art expressions of the children revealed a range of developmental levels. The delicate child's work, composed of lines and red, yellow, and blue areas, had no meaning to her. If the same comment, "This is an interesting shape; I'd like to know more about it," had been made to a more mature child, he might have related his shapes to something in his immediate environment. Jimmy's haphazard scribbles had definite meaning to him from the start. He represents another stage of development. Others drew a variety of different, unrelated objects in their pictures. Some, like David, drew meaningful related objects in a recognizable, symbolic way.

Evaluation

The teacher began the evaluation by reading Greg's explanation of his picture. Children of various developmental levels were encouraged to show their work and tell about the ideas they had expressed. Everyone was given an opportunity to show his work during the general viewing. Those who worked with non-hardening clay, powder paint, and the construction sets also discussed and shared their art products with the group.

Through this positive exchange of ideas, the children gained an understanding and respect for each other's art expression.

PART ONE CLASSROOM ART EXPERIENCES

2. GRADE ONE

Topic "What I like to do best"

- developing an art experience from the natural interests of children

- helping the child select a specific personal topic from within a general non-personal topic

- stimulating the child who doesn't know how to start

- establishing confidence in the child who is hesitant about color

- guiding the child who is discouraged about proportion

- accepting differences in the way children color

- discussing the finished products in terms of the ideas and feelings expressed

34

The children are just concluding their morning meeting when the art teacher enters. She greets the classroom teacher. Together, they wait until the children are finished.

"Boys and girls, this is Miss_____," introduces the classroom teacher.

"Good morning, boys and girls."

> In response, they return a lively welcome. "Good morning, Miss_____."

She comments on the appearance of their classroom. "You certainly are good housekeepers." Then to create an even more friendly atmosphere, she adds, "My, you boys and girls look happy this morning." They smile. "I would like to know you better. What do you like to do?"

> A boy contributes, "I like to draw."

> Another boy's hand goes up, "I like to color, too."

A few boys choose this time to assure the art teacher of their interest in art.

"Fine. There must be other things that you like to do. When you are outside, what do you like to do best?"

> "I like to jump rope," Mary Ann responds as she twists her hair ribbon.

"Come, show us how you jump rope."

> Amused, Mary Ann steps forward, close to the teacher. Then, pretending to turn an imaginary jump rope, she skips lightly across the room. Encouraged to demonstrate other steps, Mary Ann rhythmically hops backward. Her performance is delightful. Other children eagerly volunteer.

35

What I Like to Do Best—*Jean Ann S., age six*

Turning to the boys, the teacher asks, "Well, now I wonder where the boys like to play?"

"In my backyard."

Other boys become alert and interested. Enthusiasm is now well established.

"What do you usually play there?"

"I like to play cowboys."

"Whom do you play with?"

He gestures toward two other boys. "Oh, with John and Ronnie."

Through questioning, she guides them. "Would you and your

friends show us how you play cowboys?" Quickly three boys move forward. The desk arrangement composed of rectangular and u-shaped groupings provides ample free floor space for the activity. She encourages them to talk over their plans. In the true spirit of the game, they demonstrate.

"You certainly caught the spirit of real cowboys," observes the teacher. "Cowboys must be one of your favorite games. What else do some of you like to do?"

"I like to read."

"What do you read about?"

"About all kinds of animals."

"What animal do you like best?"

"Well, uhm-m-m," Lou hesitates. "I like horses."

Approximately ten to fifteen minutes have elapsed since the beginning of their discussion. The children's enthusiasm indicates their desire to express their ideas on paper. "Boys and girls, would you draw *what you like to do best?* Then everyone can tell his own story." They agree readily.

While they take out their crayons, a helper from each group distributes different-sized paper. The smaller pieces are for those who like to draw small. However, most of the six-year-olds seem to prefer large paper.

"How do we start?" questions a youngster, with a puzzled look.

"Anyway that you want. John has already started to draw a picture of himself playing cowboy, whereas Christine is coloring a sky for her swimming picture. There are many ways to start."

"Can we use any color?" asks another. Suddenly others are aware of color selection.

37

"Use the colors you think belong in your picture. What colors fit your story?"

"Red and green."

"What color do you think of when you are happy?"

"Yellow."

Other children eagerly contribute answers to this.

"I think brown is a happy color," says one surprisingly.

"Why do you choose brown?"

"It's the color of my dog."

All of the children have favorite colors. Many associate colors with certain objects, personal belongings, or special occasions. Even though each child reacts differently to color, teacher acceptance of the child's personal color associations is important.

"Use the colors you like. I'm sure they'll be happy colors if you draw about something you like to do."

With much initiative and fervor, they begin. The boy who asked about color confidently selects a crayon from his box. Several appear to be planning, whereas a few hesitate. Perhaps they lack confidence.

The teacher questions them, "What's your picture going to be about?" . . . "Where do you play?" . . . "What do you see?" . . . "What do you touch?" These questions help children clarify their own ideas.

Even after all children are drawing, the teacher continues to move among them. Her comments encourage them. "Oh, I'm happy to see you in your picture." . . . "You've such pleasing colors" . . . "You have made a fine start." Whenever possible, she responds enthusiastically to their work.

A child touches the teacher's arm. He wants to tell her about his picture. Listening carefully to the child's explanation, the teacher nods to show her approving interest. Later she comments, "The arms are so nice and strong."

He adds, "To climb a tree, I need strong legs too, 'cause I have to 'shinnie' up it." The child returns to his seat, with feelings of success and a desire to finish his picture.

Turning to the classroom teacher, the art teacher explains, "It's important to show approval of the child's efforts. His ideas and feelings must be respected. Continued interest in art activities is fostered by acceptance of the child's expressions."

Jane shows her picture to her neighbor. An overtone of discouragement is heard. The teacher walks over to look at her work.

Jane explains her difficulty. "The head is too big."

"Could you do it better?"

Jane nods.

"If you would like, you may turn your paper over and try again."

Reinspired, Jane flips her paper over.

Excitedly one child calls out, "Look, I invented a new color."

"Wonderful. How did you do it?"

He shrugs his shoulders. He is unable to explain. His blue and yellow crayon strokes have overlapped.

The teacher points out to him what has happened.

Some children are finished. Pamela wants to know if she can draw on the back of her picture. To the affirmative answer, she adds, with a twinkle in her eye, "I'll draw

What I Like to Do Best—*Michael J., age six*

somep'in to surprise you." Others are content to thumb through story books.

When the majority are finished, a few of the pictures are selected. The first to be displayed is Michael's, a boy who participated in the lively cowboy demonstration.

"Class, what do you think this boy likes to do best?"

"Play cowboys," chorus some of the children.

"Do the boys in the picture look like they're having fun?"

"Ye-e-es!"

"Where do they play?"

"Outside by a tree."

"What else does the picture show?"

"An airplane in the sky and a bird, too."

"What kind of weather is it?"

"Sunny!"

"How does Michael's picture make you feel?"

"Like smiling."

"Michael told us a great deal in his picture, didn't he?" They wholeheartedly agree. "Does his picture make you want to play cowboys with him?"

Many children indicate yes.

Suddenly a loud determined "no!" is heard.

"Oh, you wouldn't. Why?"

" 'Cause I can never catch Michael."

More pictures are viewed. The children's intent faces indicate their interest in each other's work. So then all the children display their pictures under their chin for everyone to see.

An inquisitive child asks, "Which picture is the best?"

"Each one is good because all of you told your story in your own way. You showed us that you like to ride your big brother's bike. Bard told us that he likes to talk to his grandma on the telephone. Everyone told about what he likes to do best."

"Can we put our pictures up?"

"Oh, yes. Since your display board already has an attractive exhibit, I wonder if we could show them in another place?"

A girl with closely cropped blonde hair responds, "We have some picture frames outside our door. Could we put them there?"

41

"Excellent," the teacher replies, as she distributes common pins to five selected children. "We'll have these children exhibit their pictures today. Then when we draw stories again, some new ones can replace these. How's that?"

Pleased, the children pin up their pictures. They represent a variety of topical interpretations, ways of working, and developmental levels. Meanwhile, the others hand their pictures to the group helper. As the children put their crayons away, their positive statements and general optimism indicate that the art experience has been a satisfying one.

PREPARING FOR THE EXPERIENCE

During the pre-school consultation with the art teacher, the general topic as well as the art medium was determined. Because 9 x 12 inch manila paper wasn't available, the teacher divided the 12 x 18 inch paper in half with the sharp blade of the paper cutter. Each child had crayons in his own desk. When the art teacher arrived, the crayons were on the desks and the two sizes of manila paper were neatly stacked on a table near the front of the room.

The analysis that follows gives insights into the art experience that received such enthusiastic reactions from the children.

Permissive Atmosphere

The teacher began with an informal discussion. Complimenting the children on the appearance of their room made them feel at ease. Immediately, her friendly approval and interest was felt. She assumed that all children found drawing as a satisfying form of expression. The teacher's warmth and sincerity promoted an atmosphere which encouraged free and purposeful expression of personal ideas and feelings.

Stimulation

Through the discussion of a general topic of interest, the children were stimulated to express their thoughts and emotions. While some children responded moderately, others were encouraged by the teacher's questions to relate their experiences in greater detail. Pantomimes of some of the favorite activities effectively aroused the children's interest and enthusiasm.

Sometimes very little discussion is necessary. For example, a class had fed, watched, and tried to attract the attention of a squirrel. Stories of the squirrel and his habits had also been read. Suddenly, one day the pet squirrel peered into the classroom. Everyone became very excited. With such acute interest, the teacher realized that an art experience would be appropriate and satisfying. To stimulate their personal interpretation of the topic, "Something About Squirrels," only a few minutes of discussion were needed.

Guidance

When a youngster asked, "How do we start?" the teacher wisely responded, "Anyway that you want." Then, to encourage individuality, she briefly mentioned how differently two classmates had begun. Likewise, the children were guided to associate color with a certain experience. To them, almost all colors were happy.

A few six-year-olds might not relate color to a particular object. A tree could be purple, blue, or any other fanciful color. With patient understanding, accept the various levels of development. As the child grows, he will naturally make the proper color associations.

As they worked, the teacher continued to move among them. She sincerely complimented them on each discovery or point of interest in their pictures. She also listened carefully to the children's comments. Special help and assurance was given as they needed it. Her respect for the children and their work was obvious and extremely important.

Acceptance

The art teacher showed her acceptance of the children through her way of listening, her positive statements, and her understanding manner. She revealed interest in their finished work by attractively displaying the pictures in the frames outside the door. By this gesture, she attached significance to their work, and definitely gave them her complete approval.

Developmental Levels

Most six-year-olds are active and very eager. This is their natural way to respond to activities that appeal to them. With a topic of interest, they become completely absorbed in communicating their ideas and feelings. One child hummed while another made other sounds expressive of the activity he was illustrating. Gesturing with his hands, a boy indicated how the fireman climbed the ladder in his picture.

When they draw, children of this age use symbolic shapes to express themselves. Jean Ann used two elongated ovals to depict her arms. Her fingers are drawn like a series of drum major batons. In contrast, Michael didn't define the fingers at all. Both children will continue to use the same symbolic shapes to represent hands until a personal observation or experience contributes to a change. Sometimes the symbols change quickly. Perhaps it is due to a different medium or topic. Regardless of the circumstance that stimulated the change, as children become more aware of the environment, their symbols become more realistic.

Evaluation

When the children finished their pictures, they informally discussed some of them. Through questioning, attention was given to the ideas and feelings communicated. No reference was made to the technical aspect of their drawing, nor was any criticism given to make the child feel inferior and dissatisfied. The evaluation was a positive, enjoyable experience . . . a gathering together to share and to discuss the uniqueness of the individual expressions.

Naturally, in her own mind, the teacher evaluated the developmental progress of the children. She noticed those who needed special guidance. This type of evaluation is continuous.

CLASSROOM ART EXPERIENCES

3. GRADE TWO

Topic "How I think I look"

- stimulating art expression through discussion and demonstration

- encouraging the children to respond freely

- guiding the children to select the appropriate size and color of paper

- combining two art media

- guiding children to use the art media

- helping a child to solve his own problem

(Continued on page 46)

- helping a timid child who hesitates to draw

- accepting the children responses while they work

- helping children to understand and enjoy each other's pictures

- helping the children to display their pictures for open house

The seven-year-olds wait for the art teacher. She knocks. The classroom teacher opens the door to welcome her, "We've just learned a new song. The children would like to sing it for you."

"Well, what a nice surprise."

"All right boys and girls," signals the classroom teacher.

They sing merrily.

good morn- ing, good morn- ing, good morn- ing to you!

good morn- ing, good morn- ing, oh, how do you do?

"The American Singer," Book One, Second Edition, The American Book Company, p. 18.

"My, you are cheerful," the art teacher observes. "You remind me of what Robert Louis Stevenson once said, 'The world is so full of a number of things, I'm sure we should all be as happy as kings.'"

The children appear to agree with Stevenson.

"What makes you feel especially happy today?" She glances out the window. "Is there something outside that makes you feel so happy?"

"The sun!"

"Why does the sun make you feel happy?"

"Because it's prettier outside when the sun's up."
A boy answers, "We can play outdoors then, too."

As this friendly conversation continues, the children feel at ease and respond enthusiastically.

The teacher captures the children's attention. "Boys and girls, how do you think you look when you're happy?" Puzzled expressions appear on some of the children's faces. The teacher continues, "How does Jerri's mouth look when she smiles?"

A little boy answers, "It turns up."

"Yes. But doesn't it turn up when you're sad, too?"

The same little boy answers with determination, "No, it turns *down*." He is not easily fooled.

"Could you show me with your fingers how your mouth feels when it's sad?" The boy uses his fingers to trace the direction of a sad mouth in the air. Some of the children laugh.

"Good." In a serious tone she questions all of them. "Can you make your mouth look *real sad?*"

The children try to frown. A few succeed. Some use their fingers to pull down the ends of their mouth. However, they find it difficult to prevent smiles from creeping back on their faces.

"Now boys and girls, when you're happy, what happens to your eyes?"

Sandra pipes up, "They sparkle."

"They smile just like my mouth."

Another little girl replies, "They go to sleep."

"Yes, many different things happen to your eyes when you're happy." This assures the children that there is no one right answer.

"I bet you don't know what color eyes you have," a child says suddenly.

"I think my eyes are blue."

Triumphantly, the little fellow corrects her, "No, they aren't. They're green!"

"What color eyes do you have then?"

47

How I Think I Look—*Marilyn M., age seven*

"Brown."

She turns to the class, "How many of you have brown eyes?"

When only a few children raise their hands, she inquires again, "Let's see who has blue eyes. How many have green?" etc. Now all the children have raised their hands.

The children lower them as the teacher continues, "How do your cheeks change when you're happy?"

"They puff out."

"They get hard."

"What shape are your cheeks?"

"Round," Lynn comments in a saucy manner.

"Are you sure?" The children appear to wonder. "Let's pretend our fingers are motor cars. Then we can take a trip around our cheeks. If we close our eyes, we can feel them better." With their eyes closed tightly, their hands begin to explore. Everyone joins in the fun. The sensation of feeling their cheeks stimulates them. Quickly, they volunteer their answers.

"My cheeks are wobbly."

"Feels like a cookie with a bite out of it." Others give different replies.

"Let's feel our faces, too," suggests the art teacher.

The children move their hands simultaneously around their faces.

"What shape is it?"

"It feels like an egg."

The teacher suggests they continue downward with their hands, feeling the contour of their neck, shoulders, hips, legs, and ankles.

"Now, boys and girls, do you know what we might do today?"

"No-o-o-o."

49

How I Think I Look—*Patty M., age seven*

"I thought you might like to draw a picture of how you think you look."

A few children respond hesitantly. Most of them are quite excited and start to take out their crayons.

"Just a minute. I have a surprise for you. You can have any one of these colors to work with." She offers sheets of red, yellow and blue poster paper. "Those of you who want red, put your head on your desk; those who would like yellow, raise your hand; and those who favor blue, lean on an elbow." These silent signals enable the helpers to distribute the paper easily. Soon all the children have the color they prefer.

Next, the teacher displays two sizes of manila paper. "How can you decide whether to choose the big or small size?"

Patty replies, "I want a big one 'cause I like to draw big."

"Some of you will want to use a small sheet because you draw small, then. Choose the size that seems easiest for you to work on." The manila paper, paste, and scissors are distributed. Soon everyone is prepared to start his picture.

The teacher turns to the class, "How can you use your paper to tell me about yourself?"

> "Can we color our picture on this paper?" The boy holds a sheet of manila paper.

"Yes, that would be fine."

> "Can we cut our mouth from the red and paste on our picture?"

"That's a splendid idea. You will think of other ways to use your paper, too. Work any way you like." She reminds them, "Remember that you are going to tell me how you think you look. Let's start."

> Tom starts by cutting into his sheet of colored paper. It's difficult to predict what he is going to make. Another boy fashions a shirt as he folds his red paper. One girl draws the outline of her head with her crayon.

> A child with long curls questions the teacher, "Should I make the head or the whole body or what?"

"Make as much of yourself as you like."

The teacher helps a timid boy. "Drawing your head is easier than you think and a lot of fun. Let's see what we can do." She takes his wrist and moves his arm in a circular fashion. They repeat the motion several times. The muscles of the boy's shoulder and arm relax as he grasps the notion of using freer movement to draw his head.

> "Can we start coloring in?" Geraldine has outlined her head and shoulders as well as the features of her face.

"Yes, go ahead."

> A dark-haired boy has drawn his whole self. He is starting to add sky and grass.

> Dennis centers his colored paper on the manila to outline it with his crayon. It looks like he is making a frame.

As the teacher stops by one boy's desk, she says pleasantly, "I like the colors you've used in your shirt." She does not mention the

How I Think I Look—*Diane N., age seven*

neck he has omitted. Happily, Gregory continues to finish the interpretation of himself.

> The sounds made as the children cut, paste, and color are interspersed with child comments. "Look at my picture!" . . . "I'm even putting in my cowboy tie." . . . "Mine looks more like a clown!" . . . "See my hair." . . .

"I'm putting on freckles, but it looks like I need a shave, or somep'n." One child complains, "I don't like these teeth." He shifts the teeth he has cut from his paper in several positions.

"Why?" asks the teacher.

"I don't like the way they fit."

"What could you do to make them fit?"

After a moment, the child responds, "Well, make them littler." Satisfied with his solution, he starts to cut.

Blonde Diane, critical of her yellow crayoned hair, says, "My hair is darker than that."

"How could you change it?"

"Add brown."

The teacher smiles approvingly.

Unsatisfied, a boy makes an extra picture of himself.

Everyone is almost finished. The group helpers start to collect the children's pictures.

They bring them to the teacher. Then, so that everyone can see, the teacher holds the pictures one at a time in front of the group. To guide the discussion, she asks, "What does this picture say to you?" . . . . "What part looks especially happy?" . . . . "If you like it, what part do you like the best?" . . . . "How does her picture make you feel?"

One child responds to a chubby-cheeked portrait held by the teacher, "He looks sad."

Quickly another child suggests, "Turn it upside down and his mouth will look happy!" The teacher twists the child's picture around and the room fills with laughter.

While discussing the pictures, they try to guess the owner. Usually, the child who has drawn the picture smiles, making the identification quite simple.

The classroom teacher whispers to the art teacher, "Could these be used for open house tonight?"

53

"Why yes, let's ask the children to help decide about the display of them." Turning to the boys and girls, she seeks their ideas, "Where could you put your pictures so that your parents could see them at open house tonight?"

"On our desks."

"I think you'll have a folder of work on your desk top. Think of another place." She waits for an answer.

"On our chairs?" asks Peggy.

"That sounds like a marvelous idea. How could you get it to stay up?"

"Tape it."

"That might work, but maybe you should tape several pictures in different ways. Then decide which method permits your mom and dad to see them easily. Any more questions? Well, that's fine. I must leave now." She motions goodbye to the boys and girls.

"Wasn't that nice of Miss_____ to come today? I hope we can have her with us again," says the classroom teacher as they bid goodbye.

PREPARING FOR THE EXPERIENCE

Before school began, the classroom teacher acquainted the art teacher with the children's art experiences. Together they reviewed the teacher's self-made inventory of the topics and art media used by the children while under her guidance. The boys and girls had worked with crayon and cut paper separately, but never together. The combination would add interest and variety. Because the teacher kept up with the children's strong current interests, she determined the topic.

The art teacher jotted down the necessary supplies: red, yellow, and blue poster paper, 9 x 12 and 12 x 18 inch manila paper, crayons, paste, and scissors. The children stored the crayons in their desks. When the art teacher returned to the room, the supplies to be distributed were on a lightweight moveable cart.

The discussion that follows mentions some of the techniques

and methods that helped to contribute to the spirited second grade art experience.

Permissive Atmosphere

The children were encouraged to verbalize their ideas and feelings freely as they discussed the parts of their face. A variety of responses resulted. This was evident when the children were asked what happens to their eyes when they're happy. The boys and girls answered, "They sparkle." . . . "They smile just like my mouth." . . . and . . . "They go to sleep."

When the children worked, they were permitted to draw their own way. Some of them preferred large paper; others chose the smaller sheet. The decision to use crayon or colored paper, or to combine the two media, was left up to the children. They were also encouraged to include whatever they wanted in their portraits. When one child asked if she should put in her whole body or what, the teacher responded, "Make as much of yourself as you like." The dark-haired boy who added sky and grass is another example.

Although the art experience was a relatively free working situation, there were some limits. The children were limited to the paper colors and sizes offered. Also, they were expected to work and react in a controlled manner. The children commented about their pictures among themselves. The teacher did not insist that they work quietly.

Stimulation

The discussion began with the teacher's comment, "My, you are cheerful." Then, she gradually shifted the conversation to how they thought they looked when they were happy. To increase their interest in the topic, short demonstrations with discussions of the different parts of the children's faces enlivened the conversation. The children liked to pretend their fingers were motor cars traveling over their faces. Trying to look sad was amusing and instructive. Through the use of these techniques, all the children were encouraged to respond, including those who showed no initiative at first.

Guidance

The teacher asked questions and suggested the use of a playful game to direct the children's attention to their appearance. This technique increased their general awareness of their facial features and other parts of their body.

She guided the distribution of the art materials to avoid confusion and waste of time. As they began to work, she suggested they could use their materials in many ways. Emphasis was placed on what the children were going to draw rather than the techniques of working.

Throughout the working period, the teacher encouraged the confident children to work by themselves. Individual help was provided when needed. The timid boy's arm was moved in a circular fashion to give him the feeling of free general movements. She assured Geraldine that it was all right to fill in her outline. When one boy didn't like his paper teeth, the teacher's questions helped him find his own satisfying solution.

Acceptance

The teacher conveyed her acceptance of the children in a number of ways. She was interested in children's descriptions of themselves. A child's comment was neither rejected nor ignored. The boy who asked the teacher about the color of her eyes was given special consideration.

Different ways of working were accepted by the teacher. She indicated approval by such comments as, "That's a good idea," and "I like the colors you've used in your shirt." When she helped the timid boy, she did not embarrass him or make him feel inadequate.

Acceptance was also indicated by the teacher's consideration of the children's work. She emphasized what the child communicated rather than his technical competence. For example, she did not suggest that Gregory include his neck in his next portrait. Her interest in exhibiting the children's portraits at open house was evidence of her respect for them.

Developmental Levels

Most seven-year-old children tend to use symbolic shapes rather than realistic ones in their drawings. Although the children felt the subtle contours of their faces, they drew it as a general shape, such as an oval. Most children drew a front view. Occasionally a few will draw a profile or back view of his head.

Children of this age include only those parts in their drawings which are emphatic. For example, Gregory omitted his neck but included his brightly colored shirt. On another occasion, a child drew a picture of herself and her playmate without arms. When questioned, the child explained, "We are playing kick ball." Children also exaggerate parts of themselves in their picture, such as their hair, nose, mouth, eyes, hands, and arms.

Most seven-year-olds use realistic colors. That is, if the child is portraying hair, he chooses a hair color, such as brown, rather than blue or green. Diane used both brown and yellow for her hair. She was more aware of the realistic color of her hair than her classmates. Several children tried to imitate the color and design of their hair ribbons and clothing.

Evaluation

Class discussion was used to evaluate the children's work. To help the children interpret the ideas and feelings expressed, the teacher asked questions. "What does this picture say to you?" "What part looks especially happy?" Every child had an opportunity to appraise the work of their classmates. They were guided to look for the ideas in the child's picture. Their comments revealed an understanding of each other's pictorial language. Finally, each child enjoyed the thought that his portrait would be displayed at his own desk during open house.

4. GRADES THREE AND FOUR

Topic "What I found in a cloud"

- using an immediate interest of the children to stimulate an art experience

- encouraging the children to respond freely during the discussion

- helping the child who says, "I can't; you do it for me."

- guiding children to develop their pictures

- accepting the child who doesn't want to interpret his cloud shapes

- giving everyone the opportunity to show his picture

- using group discussions to evaluate the experiences

It is a beautiful, sunny day. The children have paper and crayons on their desks. They excitedly talk with their classroom teacher and the art teacher about the arrival of some of the new birds. During their conversation, the art teacher directs the children's attention to other nature forms.

She asks, "What shape have you seen outside that reminded you of something else?"

A boy raises his hand, "Once I saw a cloud that looked like a dog."

Another boy responds, "I saw a horse running in a cloud once." The children laugh.

The teacher continues. "What does a cloud really look like?"

"Looks something like cotton," a girl with pigtails volunteers. Then she adds, "Like a feather pillow after someone has slept on it."

"That's a good description. What shapes are the clouds in the sky today?"

The children look at the sky through the windows. "They're fluffy," says one child.

"Some are skinny."

"What else do you notice about the clouds?" When the children do not respond, the teacher asks, "Do you happen to have anything that looks like a cloud in your room?"

The children glance hastily around the room. To help them, the teacher picks up a rock from the science table. "How does this look like a cloud?" She moves her hand over the rugged surface of the rock.

"It's bumpy," replies a perky little girl.

"Yes. A cloud has a bumpy edge, too. Now that we know that clouds have different sizes and shapes, let's try to draw some clouds in the air." She demonstrates briefly.

The children outline cloud shapes in the air. Some use their fingers, whereas others move their entire hands and arms to give form to their cloud.

"As soon as you outline a cloud that you especially like, draw it on your paper."

The children work with enthusiasm. Some use realistic neutrals to draw their clouds; others use bright colors. Soon, clouds of all sizes and shapes appear on their papers. The teacher, working among them, brushes against the desk of one child, who announces, "I can't; you do it for me."

With a comforting tone, the teacher replies, "Maybe I can help you. Close you eyes real tight. Now . . . pretend that your hand is a rabbit hopping around on your paper."

Shutting his eyes tightly, he draws a scalloped shape with his crayon.

"All right . . . open your eyes and tell me what you have on your paper."

"A cloud!" Paul smiles proudly.

"Yes, and it's a big feathery one, too," the teacher assures him.

Then, holding one of the children's papers in front of the class, she waits for their attention. "Now, we're ready for a game. I'll turn this cloud upside down, on end and every way I can. As the cloud turns slowly, let's see what we can find in it."

The children stare at the paper curiously.

"We may need to add something to see the story more clearly," she suggests as the paper moves again very slowly.

Finally, Peggy bounces up in her seat. "I see something."

"Good. Come and show it to us."

Peggy advances to the front of the room and begins to point to the outline of a bird. Whispers are heard among the children as they watch. "It's a chicken." . . . "I see the head."

Peggy, who is still in front of the room, has become confused. At close range, the cloud shapes look different. The teacher asks, "Who can help Peggy?" She motions to one of the volunteers.

Peggy's friend helps her to complete the chicken's silhouette.

"It certainly would be fun to see the eggs laid by such a strange chicken!" says the teacher. Then she continues, "What else does this cloud shape look like?"

"It looks like a lake with some trees to me."
"I see a flower."

"Who imagines more than one story in this cloud?"

A boy raises his arm: "It could be a leaf. That's the stem. This is the body of it, kinda. The veins could be different colors." As he talks, he searches and carefully points out each shape. "This kinda looks like a jet over the South Pole," he concludes.

"My, you really have the imagination to play this cloud game."

Pleased with the compliment, the boy takes his seat.

"Now, boys and girls, let's play the game with the cloud on your paper. Look at one you've drawn. When you find something, add other parts and colors to make it clear. Remember you can turn your paper around until you find a story."

61

A flurry of papers is evident as the children turn their clouds. They consider them from many angles. Frequently, they nudge their neighbors to tell of their discovery. "I found a little mouse" . . . "Look what I have" . . . "I'm going to make mine into a cow." Then the puzzled little girl asks, "Miss _____, how many faucets does a cow have?"

"Four," replies the teacher, bravely.

The children are still talking excitedly. The teacher encourages them *again* to express their ideas on paper, "Let's keep our ideas a secret; then we'll have many surprises to share."

"Can we make anything we find?" questions a member of the class.

"You can make anything you imagine in your clouds," she assures him.

A few children cannot find a story in their clouds. The teacher asks one of these boys, "What do you particularly like to do?"

What I Found in a Cloud—*Karen U., age eight*

What I Found in a Cloud—*Vicky, age nine*

"Play baseball, I guess."

"What do you need to play baseball?"

"Well, a bat and a ball . . . gloves."

"What part of your cloud resembles your baseball equipment?"

He points to a wavy section, "This looks sort of like a glove. I'll have to add a thumb."

"I see that too. Go ahead and finish," the teacher says as she moves toward another child.

Vicky presses hard on her crayons, as she makes irregular shapes within her cloud. "I don't even know what this is going to ·be." She colors a few more seconds; then pops up, "Oh, I know now!"

"What do you plan to make?"

Vicky whispers in her ear, "The world."

What I Found in a Cloud—*James J., age nine*

"Fine! I'm eager to see it finished."

Just then a voice interrupts, "Hey, you going to skip me?"

"Why, of course not. I was just about to take a peek at yours."

As the boy tells about his deep-sea picture, the teacher listens, occasionally smiling or nodding her approval.

Then she moves on to help Charles, a fourth grader, who has drawn three clouds on his paper. All of them vary in size. Each cloud is grey surrounded with blue. To encourage him to interpret his cloud shapes, the teacher asks, "What do your clouds remind you of that you see on your way to school?" . . . . "How does one of them resemble an object in your home?" . . . . "What part of your clouds look like something you'd like for your birthday?"

Because he does not respond to her questions, she encourages him to express himself in another way. "I wonder what else you sometimes see in the sky?"

Immediately, he grins as he starts to draw an airplane.

Another boy has found a taxi in his cloud. To stimulate him to develop his story, she asks, "Where is your handsome taxi going?" . . . . "What would you see if you were the driver?" . . . . "Show me how you would drive it."

The children work quietly for awhile. The teacher moves among them to assure them of her interest and give them encouragement. Soon a majority of the group are finished.

"Would you hold your pictures up so that everyone can see what you have imagined in your cloud?" Everyone has expressed a different idea.

"Would you like to hear more about some of the stories imagined in your clouds?"

"Yes-s-s-s!" they burst forth in unison.

She calls on two boys and two girls to exhibit their pictures in front of the room. After everyone has had an opportunity to look at each picture, each of the four children moves to a differ-

What I Found in a Cloud—*Dick H., age eight*

ent corner of the room. The remaining children break up into groups to join the child whose drawing interests them most. This child tells the group about his picture.

> During the group discussions, the children are encouraged to ask questions. Some even contribute stories that they project into the child's picture.

The teacher moves from one group to another guiding the children's discussion.

> The boys and girls return to their seats refreshed. They enjoyed the small group discussions. Moving about the room also gave them a chance to stretch their arms and legs.

> Bright-eyed Valerie comes up to tell the teacher, "In my reader, I've just found a poem about clouds."

"Wonderful! Would you like to hear it, boys and girls?" They nod.

> The children listen while Valerie reads. The poem, called "Cloud Magic,"* is about the wind as it catches the clouds and changes them into animals, birds, reptiles and people. It especially appeals to the children after their experience of interpreting cloud shapes.

"Thank you, Valerie. The person who wrote that poem certainly imagined many different ideas in the clouds, too. What other object could you pretend was something else?"

"Spilled milk?"

"This looks like a fish, if I paint on eyes and fins," says a child who has picked up a smooth rock from the science table.

> *Looking Ahead, edited by Paul McKee, M. Lucille Harrison, Annie McCowen, and Elizabeth Lehr. Houghton Mifflin Co., 1950, p. 282-283.

"Popcorn?"

"Excellent!" nods the teacher. "Perhaps you will find some shapes on your way home that make you think of something else, too."

"Can we take our pictures home?"

"Certainly. It'll be fun to see if your parents can find the clouds in your pictures. I won't be here when you return. How can you tell me about your discoveries?" During a brief discussion, it was decided that the secretary would write a letter.

Several days later the art teacher received a beautifully organized letter. The important words were emphasized by a change of color. It read:

> "Dear Miss_____,
> The children of 108 thanks you for visiting us. I found some stories in different things and so did many other children in my room. These are some of the things we pretended were other things: sponges, sidewalk cracks, tree branches, rain puddles, and footprints in the mud. We had fun imagining.
> Your friend,
> Shirley
> secretary room 108"

PREPARING FOR THE EXPERIENCE

Because the classroom teacher was concerned about some of her cautious fourth graders, she telephoned to the art teacher for help. "How do we encourage the perfectionists to enjoy their art work? Could the third graders be included too?"

Combining the two grades presented no special problem. However, the children would represent a broader range of development. Through discussion, it was decided that a familiar medium such as crayons, and an imaginative play technique undoubtedly familiar to some of the children, would be appropriate.

When the art teacher arrived for the requested demonstration,

67

the children had their crayons out as well as their individual choice of paper—9 x 12 or 12 x 18 inch manila.

The following review, categorized under the concepts basic to guiding children's art education, reveals some of the conditions that made every child (even the cautious fourth graders) pleased with the working process as well as their finished pictures.

Permissive Atmosphere

The permissive atmosphere was evidenced by the responsiveness of the children. When they played the cloud game on their papers, they freely discussed what they saw in their shapes. "I found a little mouse." . . . and, "I'm going to make mine into a cow," were some of the comments heard among them.

To a certain extent the children were limited by the art media—crayons and paper—and by the cloud shape. However, in spite of this, they were permitted considerable freedom. All of them were invited to see different things in their cloud shapes and to use colors of their own choice. They were also allowed to talk quietly among themselves as they worked.

Although the atmosphere of the room was free and friendly, it was not chaotic. The teacher controlled the classroom situation. This control was maintained "ad-lib" without rules or reprimands.

Stimulation

The children's conversation about birds was adroitly shifted to the discussion of shapes. Two boys expressed verbally what they had seen in clouds. To stimulate further interest the teacher questioned and presented an object that resembled a cloud shape. A detailed discussion generated considerable enthusiasm for the art activity.

Games were employed to stimulate individual children throughout the art activity. "Close your eyes real tight. Now . . . pretend that your hand is a rabbit hopping around on your paper." The teacher also attempted to stimulate the children by questioning them about their personal experiences. For example, to encourage him to see something in his cloud shape, she asked one boy, "What do you particularly like to do?" In addition, the children's remarks as they worked also acted as a stimulus.

Guidance

The teacher's guidance was evident at the beginning when she changed the conversation to shapes and continued in different ways throughout the art activity. Sometimes her guidance was done by questioning a child in order to clarify his idea. Specific attention was given to the child who didn't think he could draw a cloud. She also suggested that they might add other parts and colors to make their story clear.

To help one boy develop his story in greater detail, the teacher asked, "Where is your handsome taxi going?" "What would you see if you were the driver?" and, "Show me how you would drive it." By suggesting to the children that their pictures be kept a secret, she directed them toward individual visual expression. Guidance was not forced on children who worked confidently on their own. It was given only when needed.

Acceptance

The teacher clearly indicated her willingness to respect and accept their drawings. She considered the children's ideas during the discussion of clouds. None of their statements was rejected or passed off lightly. By complimenting one boy on his cloud interpretation, the teacher indicated her approval of both him and his ideas. Instead of laughing at the girl who was drawing the world, she said, "Fine. I'm eager to see it finished." Also, interest was shown in the work of all the children, regardless of their level of development.

Developmental Levels

Most third graders are happy and content to express their ideas and feelings through symbolic shapes. However, this form of expression is no longer satisfactory for many fourth grade children. Children at this age usually are in a stage of transition. They have begun to feel self-conscious of how they draw. When they work, the boys and girls seem to wish they could express their ideas more realistically than they are able. Consequently, their drawings often appear tight and restricted, with stiff looking people and carefully drawn objects.

Recognizing these characteristics, the teacher chose the topic to encourage the children to draw more freely. As they interpreted their cloud shapes, the children were inclined to use more freedom in portraying the object.

Boys and girls at this level also have varied interests. This was evident. Some of the girls drew flowers, painting easels, and grown-up ladies. The boys discovered such things as boats, space ships, and insects.

Evaluation

The evaluation of their own work was facilitated by dividing the class into four groups. One child's drawing was the center of discussion of each group. The emphasis was the story depicted by the child rather than the technical excellence of his drawing. However, some of the fourth graders did comment on a unique handling of materials. The children shared their personal ideas with each other in a delightful way.

5. GRADE FIVE

Topic | "What I modeled with sawdust"

- stimulating children to work freely with a medium by encouraging them to respond verbally

- developing the children's confidence in their ability to handle an unfamiliar medium by comparing it with a familiar one

- providing children with the opportunity to choose colors they prefer

- encouraging children to explore. a new medium in order to discover its potentialities

- stimulating the child who can't think of anything to model

71

- observing how children's work reflects their interests and experiences

- accepting the tools improvised by the children during the working process

As they mix small amounts of boiling water with the sawdust-flour mixture, four fifth grade children who came early to help, quiz the art teacher: "What is it, anyway?" . . . "Sure smells awful!" . . . "Are we going to work with that stuff?" . . . "Reminds me of the oatmeal I ate this morning." . . . "What are we going to make out of it?"

"Well, Bob, what do you think you could make?" the art teacher asks.

"We could mold people, like we mold snowmen, horses and sleighs, and a manger scene, if we had enough."

The sawdust mixture is ready for use. A few children cover the desktops with newspaper. The unusual texture of the sawdust has aroused the curiosity of the classroom teacher. She places a clump of sawdust in the art teacher's hand. "I just mixed some last night. Is it all right?"

"This feels sticky; it should be like pie crust dough."

"What can be done to it?"

"Knead in some dry sawdust." The art teacher offers her a ball mixed by the children. "Try this."

The classroom teacher pinches it several times. "Now, I think I know."

Getting Ideas From Working in Sawdust—*Robert C., age ten*

Getting Ideas From Working in Sawdust—*Gary P., age ten*

The children, who are back from lunch, look at the saw-dust mixture. Their faces display doubt and curiosity. The bell rings, signaling the children in the halls. Soon everyone is seated.

On the table in front of the room are two dishpans full of saw-dust balls. One has yellow-green balls; the other is filled with plain sawdust balls. Showing them to the children, the teacher asks, "How can you decide what color you want to work with?"

"Yellow-green is brighter, and I like it more." . . . "I want the plain. You can use it for just about anything."

The children select the color they prefer. Then the moni-tors distribute a generous-sized sawdust ball and a few pipe cleaners to each child.

Comments are heard from the group. "Ish!" . . . "Oh, it's warm!" . . . "What are we going to do with it any-way?" . . . "Just like a snowball, only this is warm."

Younger children had eagerly "oh'd" and "ah'd" at the thought of working with the so-called "meatball" mixture. But such whole-hearted enthusiasm isn't evident among these children.

"What have you worked with before that might be similar to this?" questions the teacher.

"Clay."

"Can you tell me how you handle clay?"

The class shows signs of uncertainty.

Knowing their strong interest in pets, she inquires further, "If you were making a dog's ear in clay, how would you do it?"

"Pinch it out of the ball."

"Very good. That's one way to do it." While commenting, she demonstrates the method with a ball of sawdust.

"What is another way to handle clay?"

A child in the back raises his hand. "Take a little hunk out of it, flatten it, and shape it."

"Fine." The teacher continues, "Some of us make the separate parts and then put them together. When you work this way, though, the parts must be joined together extremely well. How is this done in clay?"

"By squeezing and pushing the clay of both pieces together."

"What else is necessary?"

A boy volunteers, "Well, sometimes you can put some real soft clay between the parts and then pinch them together."

"Yes. In sawdust, it's also necessary to unite the parts together well. Often, children, our ideas develop as we work with the material." She squeezes the sawdust and turns it around so that the class can view all sides.

"Now I twisted this sawdust just a little. Who can see the beginning of something in it?" No one responds. She pinches out ears and a tail.

"I see something in it."

"Oh, it's a bear!" a few children say with surprise.

"You try now. Get well acquainted with what your sawdust can do. Then I'll be eager to see some of your ideas."

A number of boys lift their arms to push their long sleeves toward their elbows. The warm sawdust is pleasant to manipulate. Within minutes, a stillness settles over the group. Challenged by the unfamiliar medium, the children busily poke and push with their fingers to explore its hidden possibilities.

A husky boy inserts two bent pipe cleaners into a small sphere and places it on top of another sawdust form. Intrigued, the teacher comments, "That's an interesting use of pipe cleaners," and then she asks, "Would you tell me more about it?"

"This is supposed to be a little man from Mars. Instead of talking, he has a regular code system. These are the antenna." He points toward the bent network of pipe cleaners.

"Whom is he signaling?"

"Another person from Mars."

"You've certainly used your imagination." Then, noticing that his material is gone, she suggests, "Help yourself to more sawdust. There's plenty in the mixing pan." Kenneth happily scoops out another batch of sawdust with which to complete his idea.

One boy complains, "I can't think of anything."

"Let's see if I can guess what you like to watch on TV." She stoops to be on his eye level, "Your favorite program is in the evening. Is that right?"

"Yes," he replies.

Cautiously, the teacher asks general questions before she attempts to guess his specific interest. "I think you enjoy one of the sports programs." The expression in his eyes gives her further encouragement. She guesses again. "As a matter of fact, I think you're a boxing fan."

"That's right," he says with a grin.

"You could model some of the events which take place at a boxing match." In no time at all he has an idea.

Moving down toward the end of the "L" arranged desks, she sees Kersten hover over a sawdust flower with a stem and alternately placed leaves. It is flat on one side like a relief sculpture. The art teacher exclaims, "How clever! You've discovered another way to handle sawdust!" Smiling, Kersten continues to model the surfaces of the petals with her index finger.

A nearby classmate questions, "I'm making a dog. Can we cut these?" He is using pipe cleaners for hidden leg supports.

"Yes, of course, Vernon. Do you have a tool to cut wire?"

"I don't think we have any pliers. I'll bend the pipe cleaner and poke it up the middle again."

The boy with the yellow sweater is from one of the wealthiest families in the community. He is modeling a free-shaped swimming pool, a double-decked table and a lounge chair. All of his forms have a preciseness and a sophisticated polish.

The art teacher goes over to Dexter, a former farm boy, to listen to his story.

"This is supposed to be a sheepherder out there sleeping. The sheep are eating. Here's a tree with a bird in it." Dexter has used the yellow-green sawdust for grass and the treetop. Such realistic portrayal is natural.

"You've told your story well. I like the way you combined the yellow-green and the natural sawdust, too. Now, how will you carry it over to the table without cracking it?"

He thinks. But before he is able to decide, another child quickly answers, "Use a piece of cardboard. Then carry it like a tray." Dexter replies, "That's a good idea." He goes to find some cardboard in the scrap box.

A boy moves his sawdust form to the edge of his desk. Leaning back on his chair, he spontaneously tilts his head to observe his creation. A smile flashes across his face as he admires his product, a harp with white pipe cleaner strings. Then he adds a few final touches.

Some of the children make utilitarian forms. Tod explains his, "It's supposed to be a matchholder. We've got so many matches that we don't know what to do with." He points to the flat surface to add, "I'm going to put the part you strike it on right here."

Charlene builds a peepshow box. Because she was unhappy with the appearance of the lid, she is making another. This time she uses a flat surface of a square cream bottle "to get it straight."

Charlene's discovery has stimulated her neighbor to find a similar solution to her problem. As she pats sawdust around a water glass, she hopes it will stick to the glass when it dries. "Then it will be a candy jar and I can wash the inside part out," she explains.

By now, many children have placed their forms on the table to dry. They linger around the table to marvel at the number of discoveries and different sawdust forms. One of

77

Getting Ideas From Working in Sawdust—*Sharon T., age ten*

the largest forms is a horse made by Sharon. Another girl has made an elephant. A few walk toward the wash basin.

"Boys and girls," interrupts the art teacher, "Why isn't it wise to wash your hands in the sink just now?"

"The sawdust will clog the drain."

"That's right. Let the sawdust dry and then rub your hands like this." Holding both palms together, she rubs them up and down. The flakes of sawdust drop on the paper that covers one of the desks. "You'll be surprised how clean your hands will become."

The children rub their hands together. Stevie uses his ruler. Some even scrape with their fingernails to remove the sawdust. Then those with clean hands put the supplies back in place.

Bob, who helped mix the sawdust, quietly walks forward. "Look, I did make a manger scene."

"What a lovely one! You've told the whole story; the shepherds kneeling, Mary and the newborn King in his manger. That was a wonderful story to tell, Bob." He carefully finds room for his Nativity scene on the drying table. All the children have made something different. An armored car, two bears playing, and a design are among the modeled objects.

While two children continue to work, the teacher asks the others, "If you enjoyed working with sawdust, what did you like about it?"

"You can do so many things with it."

"It's easier to shape."

"It's so pretty."

"It doesn't dry so fast as clay. It's not as sticky either."

Apparently, working with sawdust has been a satisfying experience for everyone. Only one child didn't produce an end product. The teacher said to him privately, "You've become well acquainted with sawdust. Perhaps next time you'll make something you'll want to save. When would you like to work with sawdust again?"

"Tomorrow."

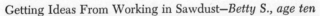

Getting Ideas From Working in Sawdust—*Betty S., age ten*

Getting Ideas from Working in Sawdust—
Suzanne O., age ten

"But that is Saturday. I can give you the recipe so that you can work with it at home."

Quickly he takes paper from his desk. This indicates a reversal of his earlier attitude. All the children want to do this kind of homework!

As the teacher writes the recipe on the chalkboard, she repeats it to the children: "Mix together 4 cups of sawdust, 3 cups of flour and a little salt. Add small amounts of boiling water until the sawdust and flour stick together. This recipe makes five fist-sized balls."

"How do we get the sawdust colored?"

"You tell us, Karen."

Karen helped to mix the sawdust and still has a yellow-green smudge on her nose. "I added a yellow-green powder paint to the flour and sawdust."

"What could you use for color at home?"

"Vegetable coloring."

"Bluing."

The teacher nods her approval. "When you return to school on Monday, you'll want to tell each other about your home experiences with sawdust."

On her way out, the art teacher gives the classroom teacher a bulletin with information about the drying and finishing of the sawdust forms. Time had been too short to discuss this with the teacher, and the children were not concerned about finishing.

PREPARING FOR THE EXPERIENCE

During a conference, a teacher new to elementary education asked about modeling media. Because both the teacher and the children were unfamiliar with sawdust, an appropriate time was set and the necessary supplies were noted for a demonstration.

When the art teacher arrived a table surface on which to dry the sawdust forms had been cleared. Each child brought a cup of flour and some newspapers from home. One child, whose father worked at a mill, had brought sawdust for the entire class. Finally, a committee of children had been selected to prepare the sawdust mixture.

To provide a better understanding of the art teacher's methods and techniques in the fifth grade sawdust experience, an analysis follows.

Permissive Atmosphere

The informal tone and manner of the teacher encouraged the children to respond freely as they blended the ingredients of the sawdust mixture. Also, during the art experience, they were given freedom to experiment.

The children were permitted to work at their natural rate of speed. A few children were still working when the teacher left the classroom.

This permissive atmosphere required some limits. At no time did the children throw the sawdust nor talk loudly. Limits were also imposed by the art medium and the developmental levels of the children.

Stimulation

In order to discover the potentialities of sawdust, the children were stimulated to explore the medium. Undoubtedly, the unusual tactility, the warmth, and the color of the sawdust inspired the children to think of ideas to express. In fact, the aroma of the sawdust reminded a third grade boy of something "woodsy." After thinking a bit, the child said, "I know, I'll make a woodpecker."

Guidance

The children's confidence in their ability to handle an unfamiliar medium was developed by comparing it to clay, a familiar medium. After the child's description, the technique was demonstrated briefly for everyone to see. In this way, the children were reminded of the basic techniques with which to express their ideas—the stick-on and pinch-out methods.

As the teacher moved among the children during the working process, she encouraged the boy who complained as well as others who were more confident of their abilities. She especially praised a personal and unique idea or way of working, "How clever! You've discovered another way to handle sawdust!" "You've told your story well. I like the way you combined the yellow-green and the natural sawdust, too."

The children were encouraged to use the other color of sawdust and pipe cleaners if they desired. By combining the sawdust and wire, some were able to express their idea more clearly and effectively.

Acceptance

The teacher displayed a positive attitude toward the children's ways of working and their ideas. For example, to the husky boy who made a man from Mars, she said, "You've certainly used your imagination. Help yourself to more sawdust. There's plenty in the mixing pan." In essence she told him that his idea was a worthy one. To others her respect for their work was revealed through her interest and concern for its safe delivery to the drying table.

Developmental Levels

The children's desire to express their ideas and feelings realistically and precisely is natural. Dexter used yellow-green sawdust for the grass and tree in his pastoral scene. Because Charlene wanted to make the peep-show lid smooth and straight, she used the cream bottle as a guide. If Dexter and Charlene had painted, they would have associated colors with the objects and used small brushes for the details. Naturally, not all children at this age are able to express themselves as realistically as they would like to. Since their expectations are so great, it is often necessary to redirect the art expression of these children into imaginative topics, such as "Modeling Something from Mars."

Evaluation

The children constantly evaluated their own work. It was a continuous and integral part of their art experience. To most fifth graders, the finished product is very important. The boy who leaned back to critically view his harp exemplifies this attitude.

When the teacher asked, "If you enjoyed working with sawdust, what did you like about it?" the children were given an opportunity to summarize their reactions.

6. GRADE SIX

Topic | **"My favorite character"**

- introducing an unfamiliar medium

- encouraging children to experiment with paper

- listing paper sculpture methods on chalkboard as a reminder to the children

- providing the children with the basic methods of handling paper

- stimulating children to respond freely about their favorite characters

- allowing children to work directly with the medium intended for the final product

- evaluating the children's work in terms of the ideas and feelings expressed

84

As the art teacher steps into a darkened room, the children finish a puppet show.

> **The spotlight is focused on two puppets on the stage. One puppet turns toward the art teacher, "Good afternoon, Miss_____."**

> **The other puppet speaks, "Pinocchio, let's tell her what we need help with today. Wait a minute, Dumbo wants to tell her, too." Dumbo hobbles on the stage. Three puppets stand side by side. Then squeaky voices say in unison, "We want to work with colored paper. Our teacher calls it paper sculpture."**

The lights are snapped on and several children raise the black shades. Playful expressions appear on the children's faces. The art teacher promises, "With such a good humored beginning, we'll have a pleasant time together.

"Then we'll need scissors, paste, 12 x 18 inch manila paper, and scraps of colored construction paper."

> **Quickly, three children pass the boxes of multi-colored paper scraps among the group. When the monitor stops at his desk, each child helps himself to some. Several members of the art supply committee distribute the other art materials.**

> **Already, the children's curiosity is aroused and a feeling of anticipation prevails.**

The art teacher writes the words "paper sculpture" on the chalkboard. She says, "I have written the name paper sculpture on the board. Now, does anyone know the meaning of the word sculpture?"

> **A boy raises his hand, "Well, is it like a statue in the park?"**

"Yes, that's one kind of sculpture." The teacher points to a photograph of a dog on the display board. "What's the difference between the statue of a dog and this photograph of one?"

"Well," the boy responds again, "you see all sides on a statue and only one on the photograph."

"Do you have anything in your classroom we can see from all sides?"

"The globe."

"These desks and the book ends on our teacher's desk," offers Carol.

"Our puppets."

"Now, in paper sculpture, we are going to manipulate the paper until we can see as many sides as some of the objects we have in our room."

"First of all, however, we must learn how to handle paper. Let's experiment with a few of our scraps."

"Can we do anything we want to with the paper?"

"Yes, anything you like," replies the teacher.

For about five minutes the children experiment. Some children begin to cut, others fold their paper many times and a few roll their paper. Two children are not sure what method to use.

"Well, how many different ways did you find?" inquires the teacher. The children hesitate. "If you wanted to make a paper nose similar to the one your puppet has, how could you handle the paper?" She nods toward the puppet on one of the tables.

"Roll it."

"That's the first word for our list, then." She writes "roll" under the heading "Paper Sculpture."

"What is another way to handle paper?"

"I've got a way—twist," says Frank.

"What could that be used for?"

"Oh, legs or the ear of a puppet," he responds.

"That's a good addition." She continues to encourage them to list other ways of handling paper. "Who has a butch haircut in the room?" Everyone looks at Chris. "How could you show his haircut with your paper?"

"Oh, I know—fringe," someone answers.

The children add other ways to manipulate paper: "Cut" . . . "Curl" . . . "Crinkle" . . . "Bend it like a tent" . . . "Crumble" . . . "Tear" . . . "Paste" . . . "Pleat" . . . "Weave" . . . "Braid" . . . and "Wave."

Then, the teacher suggests, "We have a few scraps to try the methods we have listed on the board." She moves among the children helping them with the unfamiliar ones. One boy is shown how to curl a strip of paper by pulling it over the back of the scissor blade. In this way everyone has an opportunity to become acquainted with the methods.

"What do we do next?" a fast worker asks.

"Try some of the paper sculpture methods to make your large paper (12 x 18 inch manila) stand by itself so that it forms the base for your paper sculpture. Or, if you wish, you may leave your large paper flat on your desk and build your paper sculpture out from your paper."

"What should we make?"

"Almost anything you wish," replies the teacher. "However, since paper sculpture is new to you, I think it would be best to select a very familiar topic. How would you like to make a characterization of your favorite radio or TV personality? You could use a story-book character, too."

For a few minutes, the children consider possible characters. Some appear doubtful.

The teacher guides them. "What character has blonde hair? She's in the comic strips."

"Blondie?"

"How could you show her hair?"

"Make lots of little curls and paste them close together?"

"Let's try it to see how the curls would look." Selecting a few experimental curls from the children's desks, the teacher holds them up to one of the girls. The children laugh and so does the teacher.

"Who else has curly hair?"

"Little Lu Lu."

"Yes. Who is your favorite character?" She addresses a girl seated near the front.

"It's Heidi. She's one of my stuffed dolls."

"What paper sculpture methods could you use to make Heidi's arms?"

The child looks thoughtfully at the list on the board. "I could roll the paper."

"She could crumble it and put a piece of paper over it," offers another child.

"Those are fine ideas. Now, what are some of your other favorite characters?" She invites others to reply.

"Does it have to be humans?"

"No. What are some characters that aren't human?"

"Bugs Bunny."

"Donald Duck," adds a radiant-looking child.

"Skip, the chimp."

"Rin-tin-tin."

The teacher asks more detailed questions about Rin-tin-tin. "Where does he live?"

"In an army camp."

"What are some of the things you might show him doing?"

"Oh, he could be helping people capture bandits. He's a pal, you know—a dog hero."

"If he were near the army camp, what might you see in the background?"

"The camp with many buildings."

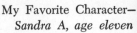
My Favorite Character—
Sandra A, age eleven

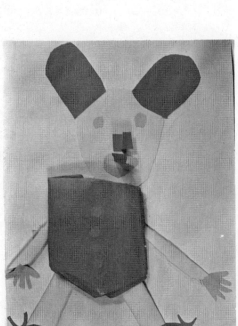

My Favorite Character—
Gary H., age eleven

"How could you make the sides of a building?"

"I could fold it and then paste it so they would stand out."

"Very good. Now, if some of you were going to make a favorite character like Little Lu Lu, who could you look at in order to help you make the eyes, nose, and other parts of the face?"

Laughingly, someone answers, "I guess, ourselves."

"Let's begin to try out our ideas. Use any of the methods of working with paper you like. You may discover some new ways, too."

The teacher circulates among the children to give them help. A few children ask, "Say, can we make a face?" . . . . "Do you think this would be O. K. for a dog's body?" . . . . "Will this be big enough?" The teacher encourages the child to make the decision.

89

Some children stand as they work. Occasionally, they kneel to look at their forms. One girl is making Woody Woodpecker and another, Mickey Mouse.

Richard asks, "Does it have to be your favorite character?"

"What would you like it to be?"

"A man—Mr. Engles, the coach."

"Why yes, that would be different, Richard." He begins to work with a sense of sureness.

Donna asks, "Can I make a cowgirl?"

"If you would like to."

My Favorite Character—
Donna D., age eleven

One girl doesn't seem to have an idea. The art teacher talks with her about some of the favorite characters she might use, "Perhaps you would like to make an imaginary character or even a favorite classmate."

In a short time, the little girl begins to model Margaret, a vivacious classmate.

The teacher encourages the boys and girls to use a variety of paper sculpture methods. "Have any of you used 'roll' to portray your favorite character? If so, what have you rolled?"

> One child answers, "The eyes." Another, "I used it for the neck." And a third, "I rolled my paper to make my hair."

The teacher continues down the list of paper sculpture methods, stopping to ask for *what* the method is used.

> Rebecca creates a little girl with a blue pleated skirt. She has drawn parts of the delicate facial features with a colored pencil. The girl's eyelashes are portrayed by two narrow pieces of fringed paper. The hair is formed with rows of brown paper curls that extend to the girl's shoulders. Rebecca is attaching the last curl to the bangs across the girl's forehead.

"What a petite girl," comments the teacher. Next, she turns to a boy who has finished the head of his favorite character; she asks, "Now, how could you show his clothes in paper?"

> "I could roll his pants and sleeves."

> "He could bend his jacket like an oblong box with the edges rounded off," volunteers a classmate.

> A boy sitting next to him is wondering about the position of the hair for his paper sculpture man.

"Well, let's look at the boy in front of you," suggests the teacher. See how his hairline goes up around the ears and then curves down into a v-shape in the back."

> Suddenly, Harold, holding his Donald Duck at arms distance, says, "Gee, the eyes are up and down."

"In that way, Donald Duck looks humorous," observes the teacher.

> The children have worked about an hour and a half. Many of them are completing their characters. Some who are finished have started to work on other areas of learning.

Soon all the children are finished. The teacher suggests that each child place his paper sculpture character either on his desk or under his chin so that the children across the room can see.

She starts the discussion with questions about the finished characters. "What does Richard tell you about the character he has made?" . . . . "Why do you think Richard feels that way about his coach?" . . . . "Can you guess who Jane has been reading about lately?" . . . . "What is Emelia's character?" . . . . "In what movie was she the actress?" . . . . "Where would you like to go with Rin-tin-tin?"

"What did you learn today that you want to remember for your next paper sculpture experience?"

Loren answers, "Oh, that paper sculpture should look good from all sides."

"That paper can be scratched with a scissors to make it feel rough."

The children give many other answers.

"Why did you like working with paper sculpture?"

"Oh, it was fun," the children respond.

PREPARING FOR THE EXPERIENCE

While viewing an elementary school art display in a store window, a classroom teacher became curious about the paper sculpture. A talk with the principal culminated in making arrangements with the art teacher for a classroom demonstration.

To quicken the distribution, the supplies were organized by the art supply committee before the art teacher arrives . . . . the scraps of paper in three large cardboard box covers, the scissors in a wooden box, and a tray filled with pats of paste.

The following re-examination of some of the actions during the paper sculpture experience helps to understand the art teacher's basic philosophy.

Permissive Atmosphere

To allow for a wide range of individual interpretations, the teacher-suggested topic was general. The few children who were not interested in portraying their favorite character were permitted to choose another topic.

Each child was encouraged to work in his own way, using the paper sculpture methods he preferred. He also had a choice of colored paper. Personal interpretations were possible in this non-restrictive atmosphere.

Stimulation

Doing something new appealed to the children. The discovery of new ways of working with colored paper scraps was stimulating. By the time a boy asked, "What should we make?" the children were quite enthusiastic.

During the brief discussion of characters, the teacher inspired the children to choose a favorite character. In a few minutes, they began to portray a self-selected personality in the paper sculpture medium.

Guidance

The teacher promoted an understanding of the term "paper sculpture" by comparing it to a photograph and three dimensional forms. Then she guided the children to discover ways to manipulate paper. The resulting list of paper sculpture methods on the chalkboard helped the children recall them while they worked. Everyone had an opportunity to consider the different methods before they began to use them.

Guidance was also given as the children worked. For instance, the teacher led short discussions to stimulate them to use a variety of paper sculpture methods. Specific help was given to the boy who was troubled with the placement of the paper sculpture hair.

Acceptance

The teacher's flexibility was revealed in her responses and through her acceptance of the many different interpretations of the topic. When Richard asked if he could make his coach, the teacher replied. "Why yes, that would be different." She reacted similarly to Donna.

Encouragement was given the children for their paper sculpture characters, "What a petite girl," and, "In that way, Donald Duck looks humorous." Even though the boys and girls varied in their degrees of skill, she commented sympathetically on their finished work.

The children worked comfortably under these conditions. They confidently expressed themselves because they knew they would be respected for trying to accomplish an original interpretation.

Developmental Levels

Children at this age are usually interested in making objects appear as they actually are. Rebecca portrayed the delicate details of her paper sculpture girl with colored pencil. Others folded their paper in many intricate ways to portray the sides of the nose. One boy crushed paper for the eyeball and cut circles of colored paper for the iris to achieve the effect of an eye.

Evaluation

During the class discussion of the finished paper sculpture characters, the teacher asked about the ideas and feelings portrayed. She inquired about some of the distinctive personality traits which the child particularly liked or disliked in his favorite character. In addition, the children summed up their specific learnings and their self-discovered methods of working with the medium.

SUGGESTING TOPICS

When children discover meaning in scribbles, broad general topics stimulate their thoughts and feelings. Good, ever-productive sources for topics spring from the children's own experiences, interests, and concerns.

Informal chatter during the children's spontaneous play uncovers their imaginative world and desires. Children are exuberant when this source is the basis of general topics. Two of the many topics that help children give expression to their imaginations and desires are "What I Found in a Cloud" and "If I Had a Wish."

Children's daily experiences are full of play-adventure. Within each child is a memory storehouse of countless such experiences. When their actual experiences are used as a source for topics, many points of deep human interest are unfolded. Much of the content will revolve around themselves, their immediate family, and their friends. Some first graders draw about a disappointment. One boy commented, "The time we moved from our house and I didn't want to." Another child chalked his, "Mom stepping on some poison ivy."

As children mature, their curiosity gradually broadens to cover a bigger community. To strengthen and expand their interests, visual aids add vitality to their vicarious learnings. After a great deal of familiarity with a certain field of knowledge their personal ideas and feelings can be tapped through such general topics as: "What I Will Always Remember About Mexico," and "A New Ending For My Favorite Story."

95

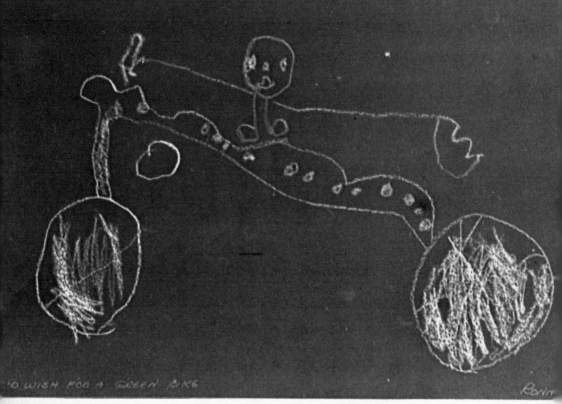

What I Wish—*Ronnie H., age five*

Regardless of the specific source, general topics must stem from children's interests, experiences, and concerns. When the topic is provocative, the group warmup discussion rekindles in each child an urge to express ideas and feelings. Each child's interpretation then becomes a self-selected specific topic affected by his individual ideas, feelings, and understandings. The following children's interpretations of broad general topics exemplify their individuality:

Age Five Topic: "If I Had A Wish"

Individual interpretations

"I wish for a walking doll and the sky and my house and my apple tree."

"Here's the daddy. Here's the mamma. These are all the baby kitty cats."

"I'd wish for a green bike."

96

What I Look Forward To This Summer—*Kay K., age seven*

Kay chatted about her finished buttermilk-chalk picture. "I'm going to New York on my vacation. I'm going on the Staten Island ferry. My mother told me all about it." For discussion of buttermilk and chalk, see page 108.

What I Did Last Summer—*boy, age nine*

What I Found in My Initial—*Jimmy W., age seven*

Turning his paper initialed with three w's upside down, Jimmy suddenly imagined the humps on a camel's back. Evidently his understanding of a cow is more thorough because his idea reveals a camel-cow. The frolicsome "original" animal is followed by two sisters.

Getting Ideas
While Crayon
   Etching—*Alvin, age
   nine*

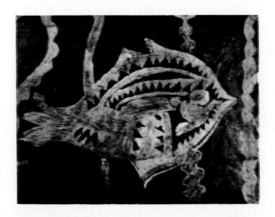

96D

"A choo-choo train with tracks."

"A puppy. A cocker spaniel puppy, full blood. Just like the one we had, but had to sell."

"A bakery hat."

"I wish for pieces of gold to buy anything I want."

"A real pony and a saddle."

Age Six Topic: "When I Had The Most Fun"

Individual interpretations

"Cookin' hard boiled eggs in the morning."

"At my birthday party."

"When I rode a pony on my uncle's farm."

"Down the hill on my wagon."

"When I saw Santa."

"Playin' with my kitty cat Peko."

"Sitting in my playhouse."

Age Seven Topic: "What I Want To Be When I Grow Up"

Individual interpretations

"Make statues."

"A lady that waters flowers."

"I'd like to be in a sailboat."

"A doctor with his doctor kit."

What I Want to be When I Grow Up—*Ronald F., age seven*

"Sell gas like my dad."

"A mother."

"I want to be a painter . . . paint on papers."

"A milkman and bring milk to houses."

Age Eight Topic: "Something Funny That Happened"

Individual interpretations

"My dog chewed a hole in my underwear."

"Last year when I was learnin' to skate, I stood up and fell down again and again."

"We're eatin' breakfast in the kitchen. Mommie took the pepper instead of the milk."

"This is my train going on a track. The engine hit a pail of water and splashed right in my face."

"My dog was chasing a field mouse. He followed him out on the dock—it was slippery and my dog slid into the lake. SMASH."

"A guy was chasin' him around a round house. Why couldn't he catch him? Because he couldn't corner him."

Age Nine Topic: "What the Fragrance Reminded Me of"

Individual interpretations

"I could draw my mother putting some perfume on and my dad in the other room painting."

(toilet water and turpentine)

"This bottle reminds me of nose drops. My dad puts the drops in my nose when I lie down on two hassocks."

(menthol)

What the Fragrance Reminded Me of—*Billy S., age eight*

"Makes me think of something I drink down on the farm to make me strong."

(banana flavoring)

"In a way, it smells like the runny stuff you put on chow mein."

(liquid smoke)

"It smelt like smoke. I'm making a picture of camping."

(liquid smoke)

"I took a whiff of something that smelt like gas. So I'm making a picture of my brother and his Jaguar. He's filling it up at the gas station."

(paste wax)

"My sister is putting mothballs in our pockets."

(moth crystals)

"It smelt like a hospital or an ambulance. Here's my Red Cross ambulance going down the street."

(vanilla flavoring)

Age Ten Topic: "Splashing Paint on a Wet Paper"

Individual interpretations

"A hat with some people in a crowded city."

"Somebody's footprints . . . a burglar. This is a chunk of land worth a lot of money. He's sneaking some of it."

"I think it looks like a sunset with two trees down here."

"This could be the beginning of a dream."

"A party with a bunch of streamers."

"A fence."

"This is seaweed under water. When the sun hits it makes different colors."

Age Eleven Topic: "What I'll Always Remember About Mexico"

Individual interpretations

"The Mexican girl ready for the fiesta, but she had to stay home and weave."

"How they dress."

"The siesta in the lean-to."

"The mountain erupting. The explosions in the earth."

"I'd like to remember the old ruins in Mexico City."

"The farmer who found the volcano while he was plowing."

"How the houses are built with sand, water, and straw."

The following topics are generally of interest to children. Naturally, not all children respond favorably to every topic.

Suggested topics for ages approximately five to eight:

- My Family
- Getting Ready For School
- How Mother Helps Me
- Where I Like to Go
- How I Keep Healthy
- What I Do After School
- What I Liked at the Circus
- The Story That I Like to Hear

- What I Did Once After Bedtime
- What I Like About School
- What I Do at Recess
- Something That Made Me Cry
- What I Like to Model in the Snow
- Pretending
- Somebody Who Is Nice to Me
- What I Saw on the Way to School
- The Most Mischief I Ever Got Into
- What I Like to Watch
- What I Imagined From Something in the Scrapbox
- The Community Helper I'd Like to Be
- What I Did on Halloween
- A Pet I Would Like
- What I Would Like to Drive
- A Party That I Enjoyed
- Recess In Fairyland
- What I Want to Own
- What I Found in My Initial
- What I Like to Watch My Mom or Dad Do
- Something I Collect
- What I Want For Christmas
- What I Am Most Thankful For
- Using My Favorite Tool or Plaything
- A Design That I'd Like on My Clothes
- A Trick For April Fool's Day
- My Best Friends
- What I Did When I Stayed Up Late One Night
- My Favorite Game
- What I Wish My Parents Would Do
- A Program That I Like
- Something That Feels Comfortable in My Hand
- Where I Like to Visit

Suggested topics for ages approximately nine to twelve:

- What I'd See If I Were a Deep Sea Diver
- Looking Toward the Sky in Wonderland
- What I'd Like to Find on a Treasure Hunt

- Finding a Story in a Seed Shape
- What I Found in My Clay Squeeze
- Exploring on Another Planet
- Why I Look Forward to Spring
- What I'd Do With a Million Dollars
- What I Enjoyed at the Fair
- What I'd Like to Be
- A Creature From Another Planet
- What I Would Like to Wear For Halloween
- What the Music Reminds Me of
- What I'd Like to Hunt
- What I Would Like to Improve
- What I Am Afraid of
- What I'd Like to Find if I Were Excavating
- Something That Makes Me Smile
- What My Family Does Together
- What I Do When It Rains
- Something I'm Proud Of
- What I Think About When I'm Alone
- What I Did That Made Me Very Tired
- Something That I Dislike to Do
- How I Spent the Holiday
- What I Imagined From the Shape of a Paper Plate
- My Most Thrilling Experience
- A Secret I Now Can Tell
- One of My Dreams
- What I Am Saving For
- Imagining a Picture in Blade Marks On a Skating Rink
- A Trip I'd Like to Take
- A Good Deed That I Performed
- What I Want to Remember
- My Most Embarrassing Moment
- Something of Interest in My Family History
- What I Imagined in a Shamrock
- Someone That I Respect
- What I Like to Ride
- A New Year's Resolution
- My Pet Peeve
- The Time I Found Something

103

SUGGESTING ART MEDIA

When the medium is *unfamiliar* or when *a long time has elapsed since the last contact* with the medium, children need sufficient time to explore its possibilities. Each material has a different feel. Some will work it thoughtfully and slowly, whereas others will manipulate it with quick exhuberance.

Children are more expressive in some art media than others. Provide opportunities for them to work with a variety of media. It sparks the children's interest and growth.

Whether the medium is appropriate depends on the level of development of the child—his attentiveness and his motor coordination—as much as on his age. Following, are some of the basic media that invite challenge and satisfaction, loosely classified by ages:

Media for children ages five through eight:

- chalk
- clay
- crayon
- cut paper
- finger paint
- powder paint
- sawdust

Media for children ages nine through twelve:

- chalk
- clay
- crayon
- cut paper
- finger paint
- paper sculpture
- papier-maché
- powder paint
- sawdust
- thread
- watercolor

In the pages that follow, each basic medium is discussed. The material is organized according to classroom teachers' inquiries.

PART TWO | CHILDREN'S ART MEDIA

1. CHALK

Suggested for children
ages five through twelve

- basic supplies

- other appropriate surfaces

- chalk distribution

- dry colored chalk

- water and chalk

- buttermilk and chalk

- first experiences

- methods of working

- smudges

- fixative and its application

- use on the chalkboard

BASIC SUPPLIES

Chalk of different colors, lengths and thicknesses, no larger than 1 inch thick and 4 inches long —— To give each child an opportunity to select colors and sizes for his purposes. A box for each child is ideal.

Cloth, 12 x 18 inches, half damp and half dry —— To clean and dry the hands and to moisten the chalk and paper

Denatured alcohol —— To clean fixative spray gun or brush

Fixative —— To hold pigment in place

Spray gun or bristle brush —— To apply fixative

Newspaper —— To stack the finished work within

Paper, non-glazed, manila and construction —— To provide a semi-rough surface to draw on

Water —— To dampen sponges, cloths, paper or chalk

church

What I Found in My Lucky Number—

Stephanie A., age seven

When Stephanie turned her number 6 sideways, it suggested a bride's face. Using chalk on dry paper, she added details to complete it. The flowing rhythmic lines suggest that Stephanie worked freely as she expressed her idea of a bride in church.

106

Buttermilk _____To dampen paper

Whisk broom _____To brush off any chalk dust
from clothes if needed

OTHER APPROPRIATE SURFACES

In addition to the manila and construction papers, other non-glazed surfaces with rough finishes are appropriate:

Oilcloth, back   Window shades

Wallpaper   Others

CHALK DISTRIBUTION

If the children do not have chalk stored within their own desks, then provide containersful of chalks that vary in color, length, and thickness. Transparent plastic containers are especially convenient because the children can easily see the chalk to make their selections quickly. Pass the containers around to the children or place them in the center of a group, if the desks are grouped together.

DRY COLORED CHALK

This previously was the most commonly used method. Both the paper and chalk surfaces are dry. Children like to blend their colors by smoothing two or more dry colors together with their fingers or a cloth.

WATER AND CHALK

The use of water with chalk is also practiced. The paper is dampened with a wet cloth or sponge before drawing on it. Children can also moisten their chalk instead of their paper. This may be done with a wet cloth or by dipping the piece of chalk into a pan of water.

Water decreases smudges. Children are quick to realize other advantages, too.

. . . First grader Georgia concluded, "The chalk is darker and it looks more prettier."

. . . A nine-year-old boy offered, "The chalk doesn't powder up as much."

. . . Lonnie, a sixth grader, declared, "The texture gets so you can see it a lot more."

To some children it makes no difference whether the paper and

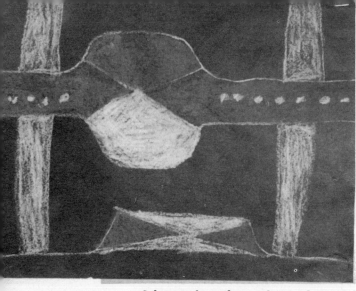

What The Music
Reminds Me of—

Stephen C., age seven

(Liszt's "Hungarian
Rhapsody No. 1")

Selecting from three colors and sizes of paper, Stephen chose the blue 9 x 12 inch paper. The dampened tip of his chalk moved in accord with the principal melody of the music. A feeling of restraint in the color and design is conveyed.

chalk surfaces are damp or dry. After experimentation, let each child use the method he prefers.

BUTTERMILK AND CHALK

Pushing a tablespoon or two of cool buttermilk over the entire surface of the paper is a pleasant tactile sensation to most children. . . . "It reminds me of finger paint." . . . "It smells like cottage cheese." These comments were exchanged among the fourth graders. In no time at all, their buttermilk covered paper was ready for the chalk.

When the children have tried dry and wet chalk on dry paper and wet and dry chalk with water and buttermilk, encourage them to make comparative judgments.

"I like buttermilk on the paper because when we have water, the water drys so fast."

"I like buttermilk 'cause it's so smooth. And the chalk is brighter when you put it on."

"I like it because the buttermilk blends in with the color."

Naturally not all children had favorable reactions. Loretta said, "I'd use water next time 'cause it's not as gooey as buttermilk." Such critical examinations of a medium provide opportunities for the children to build individual reactions and to determine the materials necessary for their next experience in the medium.

108

When the work is dry, the buttermilk acts as a fixative for the chalk.

FIRST EXPERIENCES

To begin successfully, organize the materials. Have ready for distribution the water, buttermilk and different sizes and colors of chalk and paper.

To encourage children to concentrate on the peculiar nature of chalk, ask exploratory questions: "Let's see what you can discover. How many different things can you do with chalk on wet as well as dry paper?" Only when children feel free to explore will they find it possible to invent.

Discuss the results together. "What is different about chalk? What could you do with it? How did you do it? Show us. What did you discover today that you especially want to remember?" These questions make children aware of their achievements.

What I Found in My Lucky Number—*Gregory L., age seven*

Gregory swiftly recorded more zeros than necessary for his lucky number of one thousand. "What is as round as the zeros?" asked his teacher. Before long they were enlarged and transformed into wheels of a horse-drawn fire engine. And the first digit became the side of a burning building.

METHODS OF WORKING

Children frequently discover new techniques as they work with chalk. One boy held two chalks together to make parallel wavy lines of two colors. Another boy wiggled the chalk on its side to get thick and thin lines. Terry achieved an unusual effect by brushing a moist sponge over his chalked paper. A girl cut a nick in the end of her chalk to portray the siding of her house. In one class, some of the children used chalk to change the color of their pipe cleaners.

Most frequently, however, children simply use the tip of their chalk to express their ideas and feelings.

SMUDGES

Most young children are unconcerned about the transference of smudges to the paper by their hands. They seem to accept them as one of the characteristics of chalk. When the child becomes displeased with the smudges, he'll remove them with an eraser or cloth. If half of his "work" cloth is moistened, it can be used periodically to clean the finger tips. To minimize the possibility of transferring smudges from one picture to another when finished, fix them. If this is impossible immediately, as the pictures are collected, slip each drawing between pages of a newspaper or a magazine to protect it.

FIXATIVE AND ITS APPLICATION

When the picture is completed, a fixative can be used to secure the chalk to the paper. It is available in a ready-to-use form. A variety can be made by adding water to ordinary paste until the consistency of heavy cream is reached. Beat or shake it to eliminate the lumps.

Fixative can be sprayed or brushed on. Either lay the chalk drawing over newspaper on the floor or pin it onto a protected corkboard. Hold the spray gun a foot or two away from the illustration. If the fixative is brushed on, use a bristle brush to apply it to the back of the illustration. Clean the spray gun or brush with denatured alcohol.

USE ON THE CHALKBOARD

Whether colored chalk is used for a picture or to make a title for written material, use chalks that contrast with the board. To eliminate unnecessary board stains, colored chalk made for chalkboard use is available.

PART TWO CHILDREN'S ART MEDIA

2. CLAY

Suggested for children
ages five through twelve

- basic supplies

- preparation of a water-base clay

- first experiences

- methods of working

- drying

- finishing

- conditioning and storage of non-hardening clay

- adding pigment to non-hardening clay

- recipes for other modeling "clays"

111

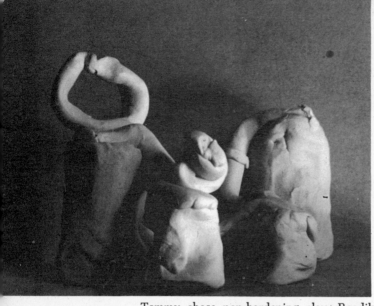

Manipulated forms—

Tommy N., age five

Tommy chose non-hardening clay. Readily forms emerged. The teacher commented, "I like this. Tell me more about it." "It's a ring," Tommy answered. A nearby classmate remarked, "Oh, it looks like a mother and her baby."

BASIC SUPPLIES

Brushing lacquer ————————————— To protect powder painted clay forms from water and finger stains

Box of miscellany such as sea-——— To use for tools as well as shells, butternuts, nails, screens, decorative design pieces of sponge, nutpicks, beads, and others

Clay ——————————————————— A fist-sized one pound ball for each child

Cloths, 12 x 18 inch, or sponges,——— To clean and dry the hands half dry and half damp and to moisten the clay if it becomes dry as the children work

Oilcloth (backside), plastic, a——— To protect the desk tops rubber tile or a large can cover and to provide a working surface

Pail ——————————————————— To collect unused clay

Paint, enamel or powder and ——— To color the finished forms, brushes if desired

Plastic bag, crock or galvanized To store unused clay
   can with a tight lid

PREPARATION OF WATER-BASE CLAY

For elementary school use, the most appropriate water-base
clay is available in two forms, (1) an already-mixed moist clay
and (2) a dry powdered clay.

Directions for mixing the powdered clay are included within
the package. The clay can be mixed in a dishpan. To minimize
the working supplies, knead the water and powdered clay together in a plastic bag. As a four-member committee prepared
the clay, they offered their impressions in a spirited manner:
"Gee, it's awful easy to mix. I'm squeezing it." . . ."It's squishy
now, but it'll dry like cement." Regardless of the method of
preparation, *if the clay is mixed a day or two before use,* the
plasticity improves. For a little variation in tactility and appearance, add dry sawdust or coffee grounds.

Some moist clay is packaged in plastic bags within large tubs
ready for use. Once opened, place a wet cloth or sponge in the
clay container to keep it in a good working condition. If the
clay becomes dry, soak it with water, mix it, and expose it to
air until it is smooth and pliable. To prepare for the distribution
of the clay, round it off into fist-sized balls.

FIRST EXPERIENCES

At first the children may need to work with the clay to eliminate lumps. To help satisfy some children's desire to throw and
pound it, encourage them to slam the clay in unison on their
desk tops. Stimulate discussion and close observation by question-

It was free activity time. Christine's plump little fingers built round
and flat clay forms inspired by the currently visiting circus. Showing it to her teacher, she commented, "Here's an elephant who
plays and does stunts. Here's a bridge and the street."

Free forms—

*Christine A.,
age five*

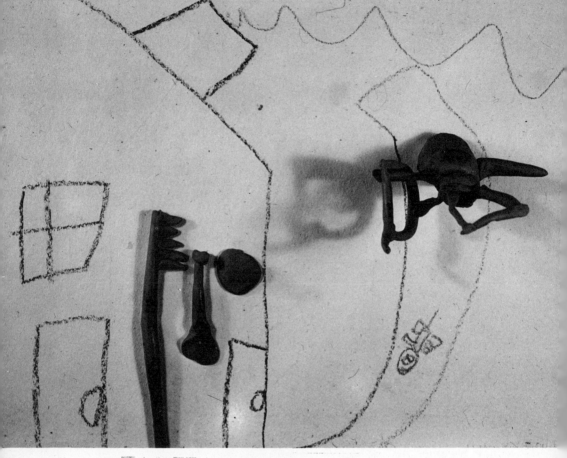

What I Do To Keep Healthy—*Jimmy H., age six*

Non-hardening clay, colored paper, and crayons were available for use; six-year-old Jimmy combined two of them. With both eye-level and below-eye-level perspectives in his picture, he developed his idea to include the outside events too. Jimmy pointed out, "That's the house. Here's my bathroom with my brush and paste and wash sink. Here's a snow man outside. He's going to saw some wood."

ing them: "How does the clay feel?" . . . "Where might it be found in our yards?" . . . "How would the clay differ from the commercial clay we are using?"

To enable the children to detect their natural ways of working, promote an experimental attitude: "Let's keep our fingers busy to discover what surprises we might find." They will then begin to twist, pound, pull, and (unfortunately!) even taste the clay. Some first graders happily exchanged ideas as they worked with clay for the first time. "I'm going to squeeze clay around him." "I'm making a bottle with eyes, ears, and mouth." "Lookit, my horse taking a bath." "This is a mouth organ. This is a wastebasket . . . dice . . . and ten cents." (Alas, the gambling instinct can start early!) "This is a boy. I made him flat so that I could hold it in my hand. He has brothers inside, too."

Some children, however, manipulate the clay with no intention to represent anything. It might be a geometric form or a free form. To help children become aware of the variety of solid forms, discuss the ones that are made. Even the appearance of some of the basic forms grouped together help children release their individual thoughts. Forms that are meaningful to the child are sometimes not recognizable to anyone else. For example, one five-year-old burst forth as he pointed toward many flat circular discs, "See all the waffles I'm making!"

METHODS OF WORKING

Usually the child's basic method of working is either the stick-on or the pinch-out method.

The child who uses the stick-on method models the separate parts. These parts might remain isolated, but if the child relates one part to another, he'll attach the details such as the legs, body, head and tail to form an animal. Sometimes forms built with the stick-on-method are securely constructed; however, they can come apart, too. When the broken forms concern the child, help him to discover ways to make them stronger. The surfaces of the single parts to be attached can be scratched with cross-hatched lines, dampened, and pressed together to form a strong link. *Slip*, which is clay and water mixed together to a cream consistency, can also be used as an adhesive between the parts.

The child who uses the pinch-out method pulls the details out from the whole mass of clay until it conforms to his idea. If not well constructed, sometimes the small pulled-out projections drop off.

Provided with the opportunity to use odds and ends for tools and decorations, children can more easily complete their idea. For example, one boy inserted the round end of a pen point repeatedly into the sides of his fish. The result was suggestive of fish scales. Another third grader scratched with a nutpick to indicate the roughness of tree bark. His classmate outlined a man on a flattened clay patty with it. Proud of his achievement,

115

he said, "And now I can punch it out." Bits of toothpick represented his hair, and beads for his eyes.

. . . Suddenly, the rippled seashell reminded Dudley of a bird's wing. So he pushed the shell wing into the side of his clay bird.

. . . A third grader rolled the side of his paste jar on the clay roll that outlined a house.

. . . An eleven-year-old modeled a form of herself bending down in the gym. Because the form needed support while it dried, she used a pencil to hold it in place.

. . . Twelve-year-old Jerry hollowed out his form, hoping that it would be less susceptible to cracks.

DRYING

Generally the small child's joy with clay comes when he models. Unless he is asked to save his work, quickly another form emerges. Let the child decide whether he wants to dry his work to keep, maybe for a display or as Mother's Christmas present.

To discourage the clay from cracking, slow drying is essential. If it is dried in one central location, encourage children to group forms that belong together. Then wrap oilcloth or thin plastic

Happy with his teacher's interest in his work, Leonard explained, "There's one night I went to the fair. I asked my mother if I could try to break the records with some balls. I broke one record and I won a cowboy hat. It was black and then it had my name on it." With the "stick-on" method, Leonard linked the concession and himself together. Through exaggeration of the arms, Leonard shows that strength was needed.

The Time
I Won
Something—

Leonard M.,
age eight

The Pet I'd
Like To Own—

Dale V.,
age eleven

Classmates greeted Dale's shapely, animated clay dog with smiles and curious glances. Through discriminate use of green powder paint for the decorative design, Dale enhanced its winning personality. Most of his classmates were intensely serious about their work, but Dale regarded his quite lightly.

sheets around them until the forms are dry. Toward the end of the drying, partially open the oilcloth or plastic. In spite of all precautions, cracks may still appear. Some children want to fix them. A rubber-based adhesive is good. Older children might want to carefully soak both sides of the crack and fill with softened clay.

FINISHING

When the modeling is over, lower grade children usually feel finished with their clay forms. Older children are more interested in finishing their work. The entire object can be painted with powder paint when the clay is wet or dry. Some children use a single color to cover their clay form. After the first color has dried, another one can be used on top to paint a simple design. Other children want to use many colors: one for the face, one for the clothing, and others for more details.

It is also possible to paint only part of the clay form, so that the natural color of the clay shows. One boy painted white spots on his clay dog. He indicated the eyes, nose, and mouth with little black lines. The only other color was the color of the clay itself.

Although the finished forms need not be lacquered, a coat of brushing lacquer protects powder paint.

The clay form should be finished to satisfy the child. Most elementary school children are pleased with unfired clay forms.

What I Like to Watch—

Mary K., age eleven

With some quick pushes and pulls, Mary rapidly captured the resemblance of a clown. The attached arms and broad stance gave sturdiness to his height of nine inches. When dry, brushfuls of colorful paint highlighted the pokes and pulls.

Many children's methods of construction would not stand up under firing nor would their interest remain through the drying, firing and glazing processes. However, so that the difference in the finishing of adult wares might be recognized, a trip to a commercial ceramic studio can be of much value to older elementary school children.

CONDITIONING AND STORAGE OF NON-HARDENING CLAY

Due to its oil base, non-hardening clay remains workable indefinitely. However, to reach the desirable pliability, sometimes it needs to be warmed. It can be softened by the heat from the radiator, or by rolling small pieces between the palms of the hands. If none of these conditioning methods seem effective, on a non-absorbant surface knead in some petroleum jelly or boiled linseed oil to supply the proper oil content. Very soft clay usually reveals an oversupply of oil. To remove the excess, wrap it in absorbent paper.

Store the clay in a plastic bag in each child's desk or in a conveniently located jar. When non-hardening clay forms are displayed, place them on a non-absorbent surface such as wax paper.

ADDING PIGMENT TO NON-HARDENING CLAY

A few colored clays are available commercially. If a certain color is unavailable, knead dry powder paint into the cream-colored clay.

When finished, the forms can be painted with powder paint.

This appeals to children who receive much satisfaction from a finished product. Mix liquid soap or soap lather into already mixed powder paint. Apply it with a brush. (Of course, when the piece is crushed for re-use, the paint on the surface slightly changes the original color of the non-hardening clay.)

RECIPES FOR OTHER MODELING "CLAYS"

Each child seems more interested in some clays than in others. Acquaint the children with "clays" that can be easily made from common ingredients. To encourage clay play at home, share the recipes with the children's parents. (One eight-year-old compared cornstarch-salt "clay" with the feel of cool mashed potatoes with salt on them!) The following recipes will add variety to the modeling experiences.

Cornstarch-Salt "Clay"

Takes about five minutes. Makes 1½ fist-sized balls.
Mix together and heat until thick:
  1 cup salt
  ½ cup cornstarch
  ½ cup boiling water
For color, add food coloring
For fragrance, add cologne or oil of clove

Flour-Salt "Clay"

Takes about five minutes. Makes three fist-sized balls.
Mix together in a bowl:
  1⅓ cups sifted flour
  1⅔ cups non-iodized salt
  1¼ tbsp. alum powder
Add ¾ cup water
For a solid color, add food coloring to water
For a marbelized effect, add pigment to the dry batch

After five-year-old Julie worked with the flour-salt "clay" for awhile, she said, "I like it because it's so soft you don't have to warm it up." If the "clays" are wrapped in a damp cloth and a piece of plastic, they can be re-used. Both "clays" harden if exposed to air for about three or four days. When dry, the forms can be painted if desired.

3. CRAYON

Suggested for children
ages five through twelve

- basic supplies
- appropriateness to different maturities
- storage
- other surfaces for crayon
- ways of working
- varying the procedure
- crayon etching
- crayon resist
- crayon rubbing
- uses for crayon stubs
- substitute for wornout boxes
- removal of crayon marks from wooden desks

BASIC SUPPLIES

Crayons, waxed or pressed_____	A box for each child
Crayons, bulk or leftovers of___ various colors	To refill boxes with individual colors when needed
Paper, 9 x 12 inch and 12 x 18___ inch, colored and uncolored	To allow children a choice of size and color

APPROPRIATENESS TO DIFFERENT MATURITIES

Most five and six-year-olds more easily hold the stronger and larger crayons that measure about four inches in length and three-eights inch in diameter. These are packaged eight colors to a box. For the child who continually breaks crayons, sturdy lumbermarking crayons and plastic crayon holders are available at the hardware and ten cent stores respectively. Older children seem to prefer the sixteen color box which contains thinner crayons with a larger range of color. If some desire to use the broad side of the crayon, the paper wrapping can be peeled off. Crayons without paper wrappings are also available commercially.

STORAGE

For kindergarten children, place the crayons in transparent containers in the centers of the tables so that they can be shared. An older child can keep his box within his own desk. However, store each color of the left-over crayons in containers such as discarded rectangular meat cans or plastic trays with dividers.

OTHER SURFACES FOR CRAYON

In addition to manila and colored construction and poster papers, other surfaces are also appropriate:

Burlap	Newsprint	Screen
Cardboard, light weight	Newspaper want-ad section	Wallpaper Window shades
Cotton fabrics	Oilcloth, backside	Wood
Dry cleaning papers	Sandpaper	Others

To facilitate drawing on a fabric, tightly stretch it onto a cardboard. Secure it with tape or clips. If the finished piece is one that requires a periodical wash in cool water, iron it face down between layers of clean, absorbent paper such as newspapers, towels, or napkins. Heat from a warm iron slightly blends and

What I Am Most Afraid of—

Ronda S., age five

"This is me," Ronda said pointing toward the penciled person in the window. "This is my house. Right here is the old shed with the flames coming out of it." She related the colors to the objects—red for the fire and brown and black for the houses.

softens the colors. If brighter accents are desired, retouch.

WAYS OF WORKING

Children usually outline a shape before they fill it in. Then they move the tip and sometimes the side of the crayon back and forth within the shape until it is completely filled. Sometimes if the colors overlap, the child is pleasantly surprised with the newly formed color. Some handle their crayons very lightly, whereas others exert much pressure. Whichever is their way of working, accept it if the child himself is pleased with his results.

VARYING THE PROCEDURE

Given scissors, some children partially cut out the shapes from their picture. Judy cut the doors and windows of a house on three sides and left one side attached for the hinge. She then folded them back to open and shut them. Others clip out entire shapes to leave them open or to fill them in with fabric or colored paper. Cut-out crayoned shapes can also be used for flannel board dramatizations, stick puppets, and mobiles.

Watch for the clues children give. For example, a fifth grader admired her paintcloth at arm's distance. Observing this, the teacher gave support to her idea. "My, your paintcloth is pretty! What do the colors remind you of? How could you make your idea more clear?" Encouraged, the child crayoned a picture on her paintcloth. The idea spread through the class. The children's pictures revealed individuality in content as well as in technique.

CRAYON ETCHING

Consists of the following procedure:

. . . Dividing the paper or lightweight cardboard into different-sized areas.

. . . Firmly coloring in the areas with bright crayons.

. . . Covering the entire crayoned surface with a dark crayon.

. . . Using something sharp such as a bobby pin, a finger nail, or a single-edged razor blade to scrape off some of the dark crayon to make the picture.

When a child wants to lighten a color, after the dark color is scraped off, white chalk or a light colored crayon can be drawn over the color. If children scratch hard enough with their sharp object, removal of some of the under color makes it lighter. Erling, age seven, discovered this by himself. He explained, "I pressed real hard with my crayon. And then I traced over it real light with my scissor."

Because solidly crayoned areas require time and a great deal of muscular pressure, crayon etching is more appropriate to the upper elementary children who bear down on the crayons. To a child who crayons lightly, crayon etching does not give him satisfaction because his picture will not be clearly defined. To spare the child's disappointment, help him learn to bear down.

CRAYON RESIST

This procedure also is most appropriate for children who handle their crayons with a great deal of pressure. After the crayon illustration is finished, the child can paint over his entire picture with a diluted powder paint. Because the solidly crayoned areas resist water, paint adheres only to uncolored areas.

What My Daddy Did This Morning—
LaDonna S.,
age seven

After outlining her forms with pencil, La-Donna filled them in with color. She used several views such as the top view of the wash basin, side view of the toilet, and both the top and side view of the bathtub to portray the room's fixtures.

123

What Hanukkah Means To Me—*Barbara R., age seven*

Barbara condensed her version of the persecution of the Jews under the rule of Antiochus as recorded in the Old Testament onto a 12 x 18 inch manila paper. She directed attention to the people in her picture: "This is after the war. The people won. So they didn't have to bow down to the idols. They went to their temple that they builted. They swept the temple out. And crashed all the idols. And that's why we bow down to the only true God."

CRAYON RUBBING

Clint was fascinated with rubbing his pencil over the paper which covered his coins. Noticing the transference of the raised designs to the paper, the teacher questioned, "How did you do it? What other flat objects could you use? From what material could you make some of your own shapes?" Clint was encouraged to try other items such as ticket stubs, poultry wire, hairpins, and paper clips. He cut some of his own shapes from oaktag, sandpaper, and corrugated paper. Then Clint organized them on his desk. Covering them with a piece of 12 x 18 inch manila paper, he crayoned until the impressions were evident. The teacher then inquired, "Clint, what do these shapes remind you of?" With other crayons he added details to transform the impressions into a meaningful picture.

USES FOR CRAYON STUBS

For a display of crayon work, crayon stubs formed the letters of the title. After making the necessary length adjustments with a razor blade, the stubs were placed on a strip of corrugated paper to form the letters. With a rubber-based glue, the title was securely fastened to the background. Crayon stubs can also be used as weights on mobiles and as hidden structural supports and decorative details for papier maché.

By melting the crayon stubs, the resulting fluid wax can be brushed onto cardboard, insulation board, and fabric. Some fifth graders who were intrigued with Chinese jade added shavings from blue, yellow, and green crayon stubs to color the melted combination of white candle discards, beeswax and paraffin. As soon as the shavings were melted, they poured the fluid wax into paper cups and ice cream and milk cartons. When the wax was hard, the children tore away the paper and began to carve from chunks of green wax. After the experience, the children shared their discoveries;

> What Christmas Means To Me—*James B., age seven*
>
> James portrayed Jesus as an adult. In front of the multicolored wooden house with a lamp post, Jesus (the Carpenter) is seated. James explained, "Here's Jesus and here's two kids going to him. There's birds flying and there's clouds in the sky. Jesus is sitting on a box." Pointing to the active children, he added, "And there I have them carrying candles. Jesus is holding the one the kids got a light from."

What I Liked at the Circus—*Peggy N., age ten*

In response to the topic suggested, Peggy created a woeful looking clown. Her use of a few colors gives the picture a unified feeling. The design on the clown's suit, hat, and cheeks adds interest. Not satisfied with the color of the manila paper, Peggy brushed yellow watercolor onto the background.

. . . Small, inexpensive pencil or crayon sharpeners quickly pare down the crayons.

. . . With fewer crayon shavings, the wax becomes more transparent.

. . . By adding wax of a different value after one layer is dry, a wax block with different values is possible.

. . . For a smooth finish, rub it with newspaper and cloth.

. . . Wax isn't as brittle to carve as soap.

. . . To insure safety, melt wax in the top part of a double boiler.

SUBSTITUTE FOR WORNOUT BOXES

It may be necessary to replace the cardboard box in which the crayons are purchased. Because of their durability, size, and hinged top, bandage and pipe tobacco containers are satisfactory.

REMOVAL OF CRAYON MARKS FROM WOODEN DESKS

Sometimes as children work, they accidentally color over their paper onto the desks. To remove crayon marks, rub a cloth saturated with liquid wax over them.

Each child drew a "skating path." Nancy moved her crayon around and around. After group discussion, she excitedly clarified a dancer whirling black ribbons.

What I Imagined
Within the
Marks on a
Skating Rink—
*Nancy D., age
eleven*

4. CUT PAPER

Suggested for children
ages five through twelve

- basic supplies

- introduction of scissors

- storage of scissors

- distribution and storage of paste

- appropriate materials to cut

- ways of working

- storage and use of paper scraps

- other purposeful activities

127

BASIC SUPPLIES

Odds and ends of paper such as sandpaper, paper towels, wallpaper and others ....To supplement the paper supply

Paper, colored poster and manila, 9 x 12 inch and 12 x 18 inch ....To allow the children a choice of size and color

Paste ....To secure the cut out forms to a background

Rubber-base adhesive ....To adhere papers and other odds and ends that require a stronger bond

Scissors, blunt-tipped and semi-pointed ....To cut the paper

INTRODUCTION OF SCISSORS

Blunt-tipped scissors are safest for young children to use. When school age is reached, some children handle scissors skillfully. However, to others a scissor is a new tool. Teacher guidance is needed to help the child develop proper coordination. Holding the tool sideways with the thumb in one opening and another finger in the other handle opening, let him manipulate the scissors before it is used as a cutting instrument. Compare the up and down movement to the opening and closing of a mouth.

Where I Was Last Night—*Mary Jane E., age five.*

How I Help
at Home—

*Joann K., age
seven*

To tell visually about her home responsibilities, Joann needed encouragement. Within thirty minutes, a fabric scrap became a dish towel and a curtain, while colored paper represented detailed kitchen furnishings. Even the cabinet doors are opened to receive the supper dishes that Joann wipes.

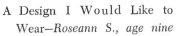

What I Want to Be—*James J.,
age eight*

A Design I Would Like to
Wear—*Roseann S., age nine*

Wanting to be a pirate, James captures the pirate's spirit of courageous bravado in his picture. Suspended from the rick-rack chain is a button that James interpreted as a medal. Unconcerned about running over the edge of the paper, he boldly expanded his idea to include the pirate's tin-foiled, speckled garment.

What We Learned About China—*Thirty-two children, ages twelve*

Interested in the Swiss mountain goat, Dennis portrayed its proverbial stubbornness. The unique leg position, the large eyes, and the powder box cheese container give the goat a genuinely individual expression.

What I
Enjoyed
About
Switzerland—

*Dennis S.,
age nine*

128C

Powder
Painting—
children,
ages five

With their clothes well protected and an assortment of colors
and brushes, the children are able freely to express their own
ideas and feelings.

Deborah was fascinated with the colorful paints. As she moved
the brushfuls of color on her paper, some dripped and ran into
others. As she develops, Deborah will gain better control of the
medium and also begin to paint recognizable forms.

Powder
Paint
Manipulation
Deborah U.,
age five

When children are ready for continuous cutting, encourage them to push their scissors to cut pictures from magazines and newspapers. However, to make the experience more meaningful than just the acquisition of skills, use topics such as "Why I Want Spring To Come" or "Things I'd Like For My Birthday." To help parents understand the purpose of the activity, attach "dittoed" statements to the children's work. For example, "I'm learning how to cut paper. Today from magazines I cut foods that I like to eat." Children also like to cut shapes from their own paintings.

STORAGE OF SCISSORS

Bore holes into inverted sturdy cardboard boxes or blocks of wood to accommodate enough scissors for each group of children. If desired, wooden scissor boxes can be purchased instead.

DISTRIBUTION AND STORAGE OF PASTE

For kindergarten children, store individual amounts of paste in small plastic containers with covers. To facilitate distribution, place six or eight of the small containers into a suitable plastic or cardboard box. Provide each working group with a box. Have older youngsters bring small jars to keep some ordinary white paste at their own desks. Each child can refill his own when the need arises. If some papers require a stronger bond, tubes or jars of rubber-based adhesive can be shared by the children.

APPROPRIATE MATERIALS TO CUT

The child's manual dexterity determines the appropriateness of the weight of the papers and other cutting materials. Medium-weight papers such as manila, poster paper, and magazine pages are among the easiest to grasp and to cut. As the child matures, a wider variety of materials may be more challenging to him. For example:

Aluminum foil	Corrugated paper	Tissue paper
Blotters	Fabrics	Wallpaper
Candy box dividers	Medical X-ray film*	Wax paper
Cardboard boxes	Paper towels	Others
Cellophane	Sandpaper	

* For some purposes it is desirable to remove the green colored gelatin or the black impressions from the film. With the help of sudsy water or a chemical, the slightly blue transparent surface of the film is obtainable.

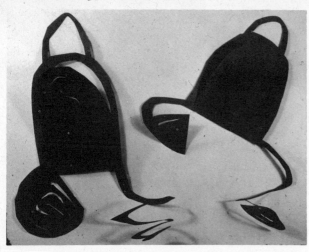

Cynthia S., age seven

Cynthia stood with two red paper forms at her ears, "I made these pretty red earrings for my mother." Cynthia spends much of her free time making things.

To remove the emulsion from the black discarded X-ray film proceed as follows:

. . . In a large shallow glass or enameled pan, place the films to soak in a 10% solution of sodium hydroxide.

. . . With hands protected with rubber gloves, rub the solution over the film until a light blue transparent surface results.

. . . Rinse in cool water.

. . . Place the film between large blotters to absorb the excess water.

. . . Wipe film until it is dry.

Because the green discarded medical X-ray film is spoiled, unused film, removal of the emulsion is easier than on the black processed film. Soak it in warm sudsy water. With the soft surface of a sponge or cloth, rub over the film to remove the particles. To keep the plastic free from water marks, remove the excess water with blotters or a squeegee.

WAYS OF WORKING

Most children outline their idea before they cut. Some cut directly into their paper without a previously drawn line to guide them. This procedure is sometimes called "freehand" cutting. Little five-year-old Mary Jane approached her problem in a different way. She painted the decorative design of her leopard with its big black, white, and yellow-orange spots. Then a round stroke at the end represented the head with black spots for the eyes, nose, and mouth. Not until she clipped around the composite spots did her work assume the appearance of a leopard.

The younger child tends to paste the shape immediately after it is cut. Some paste single shapes, while others paste several shapes on top of one another. In contrast to this, a sixth grade girl cut, shifted, and critically evaluated every detail before she pasted any part of her robot to the paper. She even used a ruler to hold the cut paper shapes in place.

Inspired by a heavily padded Oriental embroidery, a fourth grader attached her crayoned cut-outs differently. With rolls of paper under her cut-outs to pad them, she sewed her people onto the paper. When the atmosphere is favorable to such exploration, many variations in the working methods exist. For example, one boy made a paper suit for his pipe cleaner man. Another added a paper latch so that the door would open on her house picture. A girl cut a paper bedspread and shoes for her clay bed and little girl. In one class a very unique "lipstick flower" was created from magazine photographs of lipstick tubes. And sometimes children have used their crayons to change the color of their colored paper so that they could more clearly express their ideas.

STORAGE AND USE OF PAPER SCRAPS

For storage, section off with pieces of cardboard a box about as deep as a hat box. In each section place the leftovers of a certain color. Make the box accessible to the children. Some teachers provide each child with a correspondence portfolio in which he slips scraps into the inside pockets. Stored in their desks, the portfolio makes a convenient source of colored paper

With bright red poster paper and crayons, Bryan vigorously portrays the idea of going to church with his Dad. The birds in the sky and the yellow sun give the impression of a happy day. Bryan commented about his picture, "Me and my Dad on the way to church. My Ma didn't go with."

Why I Look
Forward to
Sunday—

*Bryan C.,
age seven*

What the Music Reminds Me of (Ipolitoff-Ivanoff's "Procession of the Sardar")—*Robert K., age eleven*

Robert's clear visual statement of the elegant procession went way beyond his expectations. After reading the notation about the music and whistling its main theme, Robert saw some value in his scraps. A button became a window, sand represented the road, and imitation leather formed the tree trunks—which add to its three-dimensional feeling.

for the cut paper experiences to follow. Often paper scraps stimulate ideas that the shape of a new sheet of paper could never engender.

Use thought-provoking questions to start an exchange of ideas. "How many legs do you see in this scrap?" The children's responses will invite other questions: "What has legs?" . . . "What other shapes would you include to finish the story?" . . . Soon not only will the legs be visualized, but also other projections in the scraps will help to complete the story of a never-never creature or maybe a newly styled breakfast table. By turning the scrap in another direction or by combining it with other

132

shapes, the children as a group are challenged to project totally different ideas. To facilitate the exchange of ideas, encourage some of the children to arrange their ideas on a flannel board. Such class sharing stimulates others to work independently with their own scraps. Some youngsters use the scraps as they are, while others cut them until the shape fits the ideas they want to express.

OTHER PURPOSEFUL ACTIVITIES

Construction Sets

From assorted cardboards of different weights, colors, and tactility, children cut various shapes. By slitting the sides and the middle, the shapes were interlocked with each other as well as the tops and bottoms of cardboard boxes. The children constructed small and large forms, such as animals and buildings in this manner.

Designs

For several days, a group of fifth graders brought an assortment of cutting materials from home. During the discussion of their findings, differences in the appearance and feel of the materials were noticed. Among them were shiny, bumpy, transparent, and smooth papers. One boy described corrugated paper: "It's humpy because there are hollow tubes right down the middle." The children were encouraged to make a design that they would like to wear. Some made just the design, whereas others, like Roseanne, included cut-outs of themselves wearing it. Ambitious Roseanne included herself with a round cork nose and straggling lower eyelashes. Her clothing revealed a desire for a pleated skirt and a polka-dot blouse with bracelets to match.

Flannel Board Dramatizations

Encourage the child to cut out the objects from their paintings. If small pieces of felt, outing flannel or sandpaper are glued onto the backs of cut-outs, the scissored shapes will cling to the nap of a flannel-covered cardboard. Then they can be moved back and forth as the children desire.

Greeting Cards

To convey cheer and sympathy, scraps of paper and other mis-

What I Like the
Most About the Circus—

Jean B.,

Timothy E.,

Charles J.,

Patricia M.,

David P.,

Laurel S.,

ages eight

cellany in the hands of little six-year-olds were transformed into personal messages with much individuality. Ronnie, the convalescing classmate, was the happy recipient of a dress box full of delightfully imaginative get-well cards.

Mobiles

Anticipating the yearly circus, some third grade children eagerly cut what they hoped to see at the circus—acrobats, animals, clowns, and many other things. With the class divided into groups, the children built mobile bases from which to suspend their cut paper circus interpretations. Two wire clothes hangers placed at right angles to each other was one group's way of creating a base. By twisting a hanger, a wall bracket was made for it.

Placemats

Toward the end of the school year, one group of fourth graders decided to entertain their mothers at a lemonade party. Among the many problems to be solved was how could mother be served so that she would be comfortable. Together they decided that each mother should sit at her child's desk. To add a party touch to the occasion, each child made a placemat to put on his desk. Cut and pasted paper designs were arranged between two sheets of wax paper of the size desired for the mat. Then, by ironing over the wax paper with a warm iron, the paper design was sealed between the two sheets. The mothers were so pleased with the attractive placemats that they took them home to use over again.

Stick Puppets

Because there's little chance for loss of interest, stick puppets are ideal. With tape to hold a ruler or a stick to the back of the cut-out, a puppet is ready to operate. Maybe one child will spontaneously perform with his different characters. Or perhaps a group of children will work together. Use simple stage settings and a planned story, with the conversation originated by the participants on the spot.

5. FINGER PAINT

Suggested for children

ages five through twelve

- forms of finger paint

- recipes

- basic supplies

- other appropriate paint surfaces

- procedure

- class organization

- first experiences

- methods of working

- removal of p a i n t from other surfaces

- finishing and use of work

136

FORMS OF FINGER PAINT

Basically, there are three forms of finger paint: the commercial powder, the commercial moist paste, and the moist semi-paste made by the classroom teacher and children.

None of the commercial finger paints requires advance teacher preparation. They are packaged ready for use. The powdered finger paint, packaged in a sprinkler type of container, keeps in good working condition regardless of extreme temperature changes. Also, when dry, the finished paintings are usually quite smooth, so that they need not be pressed with a warm iron.

The paste form of finger paint is packaged in a screw top jar. Because it's already a smooth paste, it appeals not only to the child's sense of touch but also to his desire for quick coverage.

RECIPES

Many finger paint recipes require starch or wheat paste. The starch recipe is the only one that needs heat. If the paint is to be kept for awhile, store it in a cool place in a tightly covered jar.

Starch Finger Paint
Takes about fifteen minutes. Makes 4¼ quarts.
Combine and cook until thick:
  1 one pound box of gloss starch
  1 cup soapflakes
  ½ cup talcum powder
  4 quarts warm water
For preservative and fragrance, add
  cologne, oil of cloves or wintergreen
For color, add powder paint

Wheat Paste Finger Paint
Takes about ten minutes. Makes 1½ quarts.
Measure into large pan 6 cups cold water
Blend in gradually:
  1½ cups wheat paste
  ½ cup soapflakes
For preservative and fragrance, add cologne, oil of wintergreen or cloves
Divide mixture in half if two colors are desired.
Blend in 6 tablespoons of powder paint to each mixture.
Leave one-half uncolored if desired. After the colorless finger

Discovering Finger Paint's Characteristics
 —*David J., age six*
The irregular center line contrasts with the repeated shapes that edge the top and bottom. Like most beginners, David used his finger.tip.

A Design I'd Like to Wear—

Susan H., age nine

Susan's straightforward design discloses that the palm of her hand pivoted as three fingers vigorously shoved the paint in a circular motion.

paint is on the paper, the child shakes on the powder paint of his choice.

BASIC SUPPLIES

Aprons or men's discarded shirts	To protect the clothes
Brushing lacquer	To waterproof the surface after the work is dry, if desired
Chalkboards and work tables of comfortable height, when standing	To paint on
Damp cloths or sponges	To clear areas for another color and to wipe off the children's hands
Finger paint paper, 16 x 22 inch	To provide a glazed surface to paint on

Finger paint	To manipulate on the paper with different parts of the hands and arms.
Miscellany such as jar covers, forks, candle discards, tape spools, paper and fabric scraps, and others	To supplement impressions of the hands and colors of the finger paint
Newspapers	To dry the finished painting on and to protect clothes
Paper towels	To dry the hands
Sponges or pop bottles with sprinkler corks	To distribute water over the paper
Sticks	To remove paste paint from jars
Thin gauge linoleum or tautly applied oilcloth	To provide a stable working surface as well as protection for the table
Water	To dampen the paper and to wash the hands

OTHER APPROPRIATE PAINT SURFACES

Glazed surfaces that do not shed their color when damp are essential. The gloss not only permits the different parts of the hands to slide easily over the surface, but, if a glazed paper is used, it also keeps the paint from being absorbed. As one little bright-eyed third grader advised his friend, "Use the slickest side for the paint."

Butcher's paper	Wood
Cardboard, boxes and sheets	X-ray film
Shelf paper, colored and white	Others
Wallpaper	

PROCEDURE

Sprinkle or sponge a moderate amount of water on both sides

One of My Favorite Symbols—

Stanley S., age nine

The distinct outline of the eagle's head and feet contrast with the feathery handling of the body, wings, and tail.

of the paper. The dampness adheres the back of the paper to the table or chalkboard. Consequently, if they wish, children are free to use both hands to paint. On the working surface, stretch the paper with the glazed side up. To smooth the wrinkles and air pockets, lift the edges of the paper and stroke outwards.

Apply the finger paint. If powdered finger paint is used, sprinkle it generously over the wet paper. Blend together until a smooth paste results. When the paste and semi-paste forms are used, scoop a generous glob of finger paint onto the center of the paper. With the hands, spread the paint over the entire surface to make a smooth background. The background is now ready for the impressions made by children as they exert pressure with all parts of their hands, arms and other devices.

When it is finished, place the painting on newspaper to carry it in a horizontal position to one of the designated parts of the room to dry, such as under the tables and radiators. The working surface is then cleaned to be ready for the next person or another activity.

CLASS ORGANIZATION

After children observe the procedure used to prepare the paper for paint, give them an opportunity to finger paint. Their immediate urge to paint is so great that it's good to satisfy it while the interest is at its height. The gymnasium, the multi-purpose room, and even some classrooms have enough working surfaces for the entire class to work freely.

However, if the space and the supplies are limited, a group of four to six children can work at the chalkboard or at a large table of appropriate height. Place the water and paint in the center of the table or in the chalk trays. The other children like to watch the *first group*. With successive groups, the values of observance and the interest span soon decrease. The others can then work with other art media or another area of learning as they wait for their turn.

FIRST EXPERIENCES

Talk about the various parts of the hands, arms, and other miscellany that can be used for finger painting; for example, the palm, the fist, a tape spool, and others. To provoke a variety of responses, question them; for example, "If you were to paint with some of these parts, how would you move them on your paper?" A small six-year-old contributed, "Oh, in a pointed line," as he simultaneously drew a horizontal zigzag line in the air with his finger.

What It Reminds Me of—*Monica J., age eleven*

Her desk was placed so that she could work from all sides. Monica whirled the side of her arm and hand on the paper covered with black finger paint. Looking at the impressions, she proclaimed, "It reminds me of turning. It's a wheel turning fast." She clarified her idea with additional work.

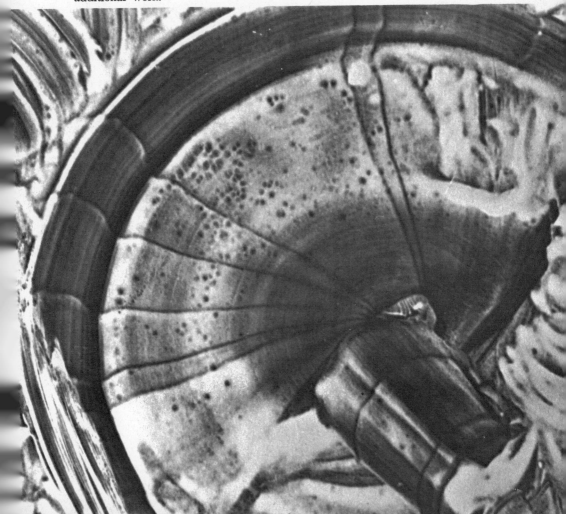

Exploring With Finger Paint—

Gary M., age twelve

Gary's handling brought admiration from his classmates. Here is a chorus line made with lower arm impressions!

As movements are suggested, encourage the children to try them by using the different parts of their hands on the surface of their desks. If, however, the painting surface will be upright, the air is more appropriate than the horizontal desk surface.

Often, music in the background relaxes the children as they paint. Suggest, "As you paint, move your body or hands to pretend that you waltz or skate to the music."

METHODS OF WORKING

Methods vary. Some children work with both hands, whereas others use one. Young boys and girls frequently use their finger tips. A few use many parts as they work. Some children clench their fist and use the side of their hand for painting. The palm of the hand, the back of the hand, the heel of the hand, the knuckles, the base of the palm and thumb are also possibilities. Although the side of the arm and the elbow can be used, young children find it difficult to control these parts without getting paint on their clothing and on others. More than one color at a time can confuse some young boys and girls. However, the more experienced children like to clear an area with a damp cloth in preparation for another color or spread colors over one another.

Fabric or paper cutouts added on top of the finger painting also enables some children to clarify their ideas better. Various items such as nails, sponges, or shells can be used to make impressions on the painting. A sixth grader started to paint at the top of his paper, and moved downward. Thus, he was able to achieve an effect of distance in his painting. Rudy, who was using yellow finger paint, added orange to make his color darker. Other children push their paint firmly in order to make their design show up well.

REMOVAL OF PAINT FROM OTHER SURFACES

Use clear water to sponge the paint from skin. Even though children's clothes are protected, occasionally areas other than the paper have paint on them. A cotton fabric should be soaked in clear, cold water before it is washed. Brush the paint from a woolen fabric when it is dry.

FINISHING AND USE OF WORK

If ironing is needed, when dry, press some of them simultaneously on the reverse side with a warm iron. Finger paint designs and illustrations are suitable for wall and table displays. However, the designs can be used for other purposeful classroom activities. Maybe the "dittoed" reports of fathers' classroom discussions about their occupations require covers. Possibly the backs of the chalkboard erasers need a little color. Perhaps the finger paintings will be cut, formed, and pasted to make a meaningful picture or sculpture. Discuss it with the children to determine their use. If a washable surface is desired, apply a coat of brushing lacquer.

143

6. PAPER SCULPTURE

Suggested for children

ages nine through twelve

- basic supplies

- introduction

- ways of working

- demonstration of techniques

- other appropriate materials

- using a three-dimensional form

- other purposeful activities

144

BASIC SUPPLIES

Paper, manila and colored construction, 9 x 12 inch and 12 x 18 inch	To allow children choice of size and color
Paste and stapler	To secure papers together
Scissors	To cut the paper

INTRODUCTION

In addition to the approach described in the sixth grade art experience, paper sculpture can also emerge naturally from discussion and participation in traditional Chinese paper folds. Because older children are curious about children's activities in the world-wide community, this form of sculpture usually captivates their interest. To invite further exploration after some paper-folding experiences, question them: "Now that we know some Chinese folds, in what other ways can we handle paper?"

WAYS OF WORKING

Paper sculpture is a method of handling dry paper so that it appears three-dimensional. Paste or a staple is used to attach one dry piece of paper to another. It differs from papier-maché, which requires small strips of paper coated with paste and afterwards placed on top of another in layers. The finished papier-maché form is stronger than the lightweight paper sculpture.

A few suggestions from the children is a good beginning. As the children work, they discover other ways to handle paper. Their discoveries are more meaningful than teacher-imposed ones. However, if disinterest due to lack of discovery arises, suggest a few words to stimulate further experimentation. Weave, roll, cut, tear, paste, curl, twist, fringe, braid, pleat, staple, punch, crush, sew, fold, and tie are some of the methods children have

What I Imagined in a Paper Plate—

Crystal D., age nine

Crystal defined the neck and jaw by cutting out parts of the plate. The eyes spring out to add interest to the benign expression.

Illustrating
My Favorite
Story—

*Dianne L.,
age nine*

used. Some children cut, bend and paste the paper to form a series
of chains for hair. One meticulous child used the edge of her
ruler to tear her paper for long curls. A fourth grader rolled her
paper and secured it with paste to make a king and queen. As she
slipped her hands up through the forms, she said, "When I get
home I'm going to have a puppet show." Then, wiggling her fingers through some holes on the side, she explained, "I'm going to
use real live fingers for the puppets' arms."

DEMONSTRATION OF TECHNIQUES

Some children want to see how a certain effect is achieved. To
help the children grasp a technique, the teacher or child demon-
strator should stand or sit with her back to the class or to the
group of children. With her arms lifted slightly, the children will
be able to follow the demonstration better over her shoulder.
After the demonstration, naturally the interested ones will try
their own variation of it.

OTHER APPROPRIATE MATERIALS

With an assortment of materials, the child can decide whether
he will use a flat piece of paper as the base or an already constructed three-dimensional form.

Cellophane	Cone-shaped spools	Sandpaper
Cereal and salt	Corrugated paper	Soda straws
boxes	Egg cartons	Tissue paper
Chocolate candy	Mailing tubes	Wax paper
cups	Paper bags	Want-ad section
Colorful magazine	Paper towels	Others
pages	Pleated muffin cups	

146

USING A THREE-DIMENSIONAL FORM

Let the form suggest the specific topic. To open up a conversation, a fourth grade teacher questioned her class as they viewed a shoe box, "What does this shape remind you of?"

The children's ideas varied:

... Lynn concluded , "It sort of reminds me of the ore boat I saw if I added some things to it."

... "Turned long way up, it makes me think of a face."

... "It looks like an easel," Jane commented.

... "I think it could be a knapsack—the one I lay down on when I fish."

Soon the classroom was filled with working noises. The discussion had stimulated each child to work in his own way. For example, one boy used mailing tubes to form legs for his animal. To attach them to the gift box body, he pasted colored paper strips to make them fit flat against the body. The rolled paper neck for his animal was stapled to the box. To make the head, he folded his paper into a triangular shape and pasted it onto the neck. Soon his animal was complete with paper sculpture ears, eyes, mane, nose and even a fringed tail.

OTHER PURPOSEFUL ACTIVITIES
Brochures

Because the fourth graders were responsible for a hall exhibit, the class used book week as a theme. The topic was launched with this question: "How might you sell your favorite story to a friend who is not apt to read it without knowing something about it?"

What I Imagined in a Paper Plate—*Roland W., age ten*

The roundness of the paper plate reminded Roland of a spider and his web. His dexterity is reflected in the woven paper strips. The color and the decorative design of the spider make it the center point of interest.

147

After a short discussion, they proceeded to answer the question graphically in their own way. Diane folded a 9 x 12 inch manila paper for an advertising brochure. Improvising as she worked on the inside, Diane deserted the base line to group the sister characters from *"Little Women."* She pasted the cut-out main characters on springs to make them pop out. Her careful observations are revealed through the details of the characters and the interior appointments.

Naturally, other children solved the problem differently. In contrast to the brochure idea, some sculptured illustrations.

Greeting Cards

"How could you fold your paper for this greeting card?" This thought-stimulating question provoked a variety of folds, from an accordion pleat to a traditional French fold. To encourage additional original thought, the placement of the design and sentiment was also discussed. Then to direct the class attention to the purpose of the greeting card, the teacher inquired, "What is something funny that might happen at your house on Christmas Eve that would be appropriate for greetings to your parents?"

The children swayed with laughter as some gave their ideas: "I could tickle Santa's feet as he comes down the chimney." Another boy piped up, "The Christmas tree might chase Santa out of the house."

The discussion was then guided to include other Christmas symbols. Delighted by this approach, the children responded freely, and certainly the parents enjoyed the original thought revealed in the finished paper sculpture greeting cards.

Mobiles

One spring day after making paper sculpture fishermen, boats, and the class's "limit" of fancy fish, the children grouped and arranged them to form several mobiles. Some children tied them onto branches, wires, or pieces of cardboard. Suspended from the light fixtures, the air currents subtly moved the paper sculptured forms. After two weeks of display in their own room, they gladly hung them by the principal's office for everyone to enjoy.

Murals

With the enthusiasm and interest for their study of China at its height, the children began to make a mural. The working groups were formed on the basis of the aspect of China of most interest to them. Each group chose the size of paper they liked to work on. Their knowledge of paper sculpture and China helped them quickly to change the two-dimensional quality of the paper into significant shapes and forms. When done, they tentatively arranged their paper sculpture illustrations that included people, homes, vegetation and others on a movable display board. Of course, some "I-can-do-it-better" attitudes existed, but when finished, the feeling among the children was that they couldn't have accomplished such a task alone. The diverse ideas and methods of working blended into a mural of beauty and expression.

Treat Boxes

As the first graders waited for the buses to take them to the farm, some sixth graders ran toward them with boxes with bouncy forms on top. Upon closer observation, one had smug-looking never-never birds on top, another displayed sculptured imaginative floral blossoms, and the third box was an all-over design of pleated and crushed paper.

This all happened after some of the sixth graders had discussed their younger brothers' and sisters' forthcoming trip to the farm. Because they ought to have food to take along, the sixth graders decorated treat boxes with paper sculpture forms for them. Inside the boxes were cookies wrapped in colored tissue paper matching a color on the cover of the box. Needless to say, the young children were excited and pleased with their treat boxes.

Someone I Would Like to Meet—*Charles T., age eleven*

Charles rolled his paper to form Queen Victoria. Minute pleats make the sceptre and the crown. Also were used: fringing, folding, cutting, and pasting.

7. PAPIER-MACHÉ

Suggested for children

ages nine through twelve

- basic supplies

- bases for papier-maché

- tearing papier-maché strips

- class organization

- source and application of flour paste

- application of papier-maché strips

- removal of base

- finishing

- paper pulp

BASIC SUPPLIES

Brushing lacquer	To protect the painted surface, if desired
Flour paste of the consistency of thick cream in a shallow jar	To bind the pieces or strips of paper together
Newspaper, colored and uncolored, torn into pieces or strips	To form the papier-maché pulp, the strips, and the dry stuffing
Newspapers	To protect the desktops
Odds and ends such as poultry wire, buttons, mailing tubes, string, dowel rods, cardboard boxes, fabrics and others	To use in the construction of the base and the decoration
Paint, enamel, or powder	To decorate the finished form
Paper towels, torn into pieces or strips	To provide a yellow-white, absorbent finishing layer, if desired
Pliers, diagonal cutting	To cut wire
Saw, coping	To cut the cardboard forms to the desired shape and size for the base
Scissors	To cut the string and cardboard
String and stapler	To join parts of the base together

BASES FOR PAPIER-MACHÉ

Children improvise and alter the bases as they manipulate them to express their ideas and feelings. Anything that works is a good base.

Fruit Used As a Base—*three children, ages nine*

The children powder-painted their hollowed papier-maché forms. When the paint was dry, simple designs were added. The sturdiness of the paper shells insured a safe trip home.

151

Bags, stuffed paper	Newspaper, rolled and
Balloons, inflated	crushed
Cardboard boxes	Paper plates
Children's faces	Vegetables
Clay	Wires, pipe cleaners,
Dowel rods	poultry or stove pipe
Eggs, shells, glass or plastic	Others
Light bulbs	
Mailing tubes	

After the members of a fifth grade class understood the idea of papier-maché, they discussed what could be used to build a base. The "base" is the form before it is given finishing details. The next day, the children came to school with quite an assortment. Because it was their first papier-maché experience, each child tested the medium in many ways. One child rolled poultry wire to represent an animal's body. A mailing tube for the head was complete with an inserted stovepipe wire neck. He interlocked two "U" shaped rolls of paper through the wire body for legs. With everything assembled moments later, he looped string around the top of the front and back legs to make them stand erect. The animal was ready for the crushed paper stuffing.

In contrast, another child inflated a balloon for the base of a puppet's head. He taped on a cardboard nose and wooden splinters for eyebrows. The ears were formed by pieces of pipe cleaner held in place with tape. To give body to the facial details, Ralph padded them with paper excelsior.

Another child twisted and bent discarded telephone wires to achieve a skeleton. She covered the wires with newspaper so that the papier-maché strips would adhere more easily to the wires.

A Character I Enjoy—"Pappy" *by Martha M.,* "Mammy" *by Roberta R., ages ten*

Martha and Roberta were eager to dramatize Pappy and Mammy Yokum. Old light bulbs formed the bases for the papier-maché heads.

152

To give it body, crushed wads of paper were tied to cover parts of the skeleton.

If the base is to be removed later such as clay, a plastic egg, a light bulb, or a vegetable, grease it with petroleum jelly or wax it for easy removal. When a child's face is the base, protect it with gauze or a nylon stocking with appropriately placed openings for the child's eyes, nose and mouth. Because it holds the form of the children's faces, use brown kraft gummed tape instead of newspaper strips.

TEARING PAPIER-MACHÉ STRIPS

To cover the base and stuffing, newspaper pieces or strips are needed.

Of course, any method of tearing the newspaper strips is acceptable. However, some methods are quicker. For example: Place the folded edge of the newspaper toward the top of the desk. With one hand securely on the paper, the child, with his other hand, can tear many strips of paper simultaneously.

The width of the strips depends on the size of the form to be covered. A lemon would require smaller strips than a life-sized person. However, even to cover one form, strips of different sizes are often needed.

CLASS ORGANIZATION

When children build their bases simultaneously, an exchange of ideas results on an unorganized basis. However, for the paste and paint processes of the more lengthy activities, it is often more practical to have the children work in groups so that they can share materials better. Organize two tables: one for the *paste process* and the other for the *paint activities*. Group the necessary supplies in the middle of each table. Such a class organization permits one group of children to benefit from another's experiences.

Some teachers, however, prefer to have the children finish the papier-maché activity at their own desks. With the supplies distributed to each individual, the whole class pastes simultaneously and when dry, finishes them.

SOURCE AND APPLICATION OF FLOUR PASTE

To make the paste, shake flour and water together until it reaches the consistency of thick cream. Whether the children bring their own already-mixed flour paste from home depends on

153

My Favorite Nursery Rhyme—

Robert N., age eleven

Robert believes that physical strength character-
izes "The Farmer in the Dell." Note the exaggerated arms. All of his attire—blue overall and
flesh-colored skin—reveal Robert's desire to be
realistic.

the length of the activity. For big activities such as life-sized
forms that extend over a longer period of time, mix the paste as
the children need it or add oil of clove to keep it sweet. Gradually
pour flour or wheat paste into water until a thick cream consistency is reached.

Dip the paper strips into the flour paste so that it simultaneously coats both sides of the paper strips. If the index finger of
one hand is used to hold the strip in the paste solution, with the
other hand the child can pull the strip out, scraping the edge of
the container to remove surplus paste and to smooth it.

APPLICATION OF PAPIER-MACHÉ STRIPS

Attach the paper strips to the base by *overlapping* the edges
and by pressing them down to fit the contour of the form smooth-
ly. If a layer is saturated with paste, the child can apply dry strips
of paper for the next layer. Papier-maché is easier to handle if it
is not slippery with paste.

About three or four layers of pasted strips can be applied
without danger of mildew. The application of more strips extends
the length of the drying time. If not dry within two or three
days, the form is apt to mold. Colored and uncolored newspaper
applied alternately helps children count the layers. Four layers
builds about a 1/16 inch paper wall. When dry, add more layers
of paper strips or more stuffing for additional thickness, if desired.

REMOVAL OF THE BASE

When thoroughly dry, if the base—such as an egg, light bulb,
or vegetable—is to be removed, use a paring knife to cut lengthwise around the form. With the paper shell in two pieces, remove
the inside base. Some children may wish to make their form into
a toy for a little brother or sister. Stones, marbles, or bells can be
placed inside the form to give it a tinkling sound when shaken.

Bind the two halves together with papier-maché strips. Finish the layer, smoothing carefully to hide the seam.

When papier-maché forms are to be used as ornaments on gift packages, a display board or on a tree, insert a hairpin hanger into one end of the form. Bend the hairpin ends outward into hooks before insertion. Use the tip of a paring knife to cut the opening for the hanger.

FINISHING

The child creator determines whether the papier-maché is to remain an uncovered gray-white. For a yellow-white background, apply torn strips from a roll of paper towels. The dried papier-maché form can be finished with crayon, enamel or powder paint, fabric, paper sculpture, and others.

Naturalistic-minded children use colors to match their idea as nearly as possible. For instance, a fourth grade boy painted his kangaroo with yellow powder paint. Carefully he cut shapes from brown corduroy for the spots. In the same class, Andrea combined cardboard and household tape for a top hat and a discarded eye glass for the monocle to add personality to her imaginative duck.

Some children crayon or paint an all-over or border design on the unpainted background. If the crayon is washed over with a diluted powder paint, the paint adheres only to the uncrayoned surfaces. This process is known as *crayon resist.*

Others paint the background first and then the decorative design. After the entire background is painted, start with the lightest color of the decorative design.

The perfectionists often prefer to preplan their designs. If paper sculptured details are included in the plan, they are usually added last.

Something Inspired by the Inca Indians—

Stephen N., age twelve

To a brown kraft, gummed-tape model of his own face, Stephen applied papier-maché strips. Inspired by Inca designs, he selected miscellany from mother's scrap drawer to enliven his interpretation of the god of agriculture.

PAPER PULP

Paper pulp has characteristics that are distinctly its own, but it is handled much like clay. Because it lacks the plasticity of clay, provide toothpicks for those children who use the stick-on method. Eleven-year-old Joanie concluded enthusiastically, "It doesn't make your hands dry out like other clays, but otherwise, they're nearly the same." Paper pulp, however, can also be applied to a base if the base doesn't need to be removed later. Its look and feel are bumpy and, when dry, it's surprisingly light in weight.

Prepare paper pulp by soaking small pieces of torn newspaper in warm water for about thirty minutes. Pour off the excess water. Then tear the newspaper into smaller pieces and squeeze until a smooth pulp results. As a nine-year-old described it, "Until it's like wet tissue paper." Drain off the excess moisture. Add thick flour paste or mucilage to the paper pulp. Test it until the desired consistency is reached. If it is too sticky, add more paper; if too dry, more paste is needed. For a preservative, mix in a drop of oil of clove or wintergreen.

CHILDREN'S ART MEDIA

8. POWDER PAINT

Suggested for children
ages five through twelve

- basic supplies

- appropriate surfaces

- introduction and s t o r a g e of brushes

- mixing the paint

- suitable classroom painting areas

- organization of supplies

- drying the paintings

- painting on three-dimensional forms

- paint "printing"

157

BASIC SUPPLIES

For Painting Pictures

Brushes and other tools such as ....To apply paint
shaving brushes, sponges, forks,
and broom corn

Containers, plastic, metal or ....To hold paint and to dis-
waxed cardboard ....tribute and collect
paint jars

Easel, chalkboards ....To permit children to
or table and floor surfaces ....paint on firm upright
and horizontal surfaces

Linoleum, thin gauge ....To protect the floor surfaces under the easel
or chalkboards from
paint

Nails, inserted on easel or ....To secure paper to the
masking tape ....easel and chalkboard

Paint, powder mixed with water ....To minimize the paint
to a thick consistency ....drips

Paper, newsprint 24 x 36 inch, ...To paint on
printed or unprinted

Shirts, men's discarded or aprons ....To protect children's
clothes

Sponges or damp cloths ....To remove paint drips

Sticks ....To stir paint

Water ....To clean brushes and to
mix paint

For Painting Applied Designs Onto Three-Dimensional Forms

Brushes ....To apply paint

Brushing lacquer ....To protect finished forms
from fingerprints and
waterstains, if desired

Containers, shallow ....To hold paint

Paint powder, medium consistency ....To provide a choice of
in a variety of colors ....color

Water ....To clean brushes and to
mix paint

For Paint "Printing"

Jar lids or saucers ....To hold paint

158

Odds and ends to print with such as pipe cleaners, erasers, potatoes, inner tubes, box covers, and others	To stamp onto the paper to get an impression of the painted part
Paint, powder, medium consistency of various colors	To provide a choice of color
Brushes and paper towel pads, folded and dampened	To apply paint. Fit the paper towel into shallow paint containers as a printing pad
Paper, manila, newsprint, or poster of several sizes and colors	To provide a choice of size and color of paper to print on
Scissors and knives with serrated edges	To make the printing surfaces smooth and varied in their shape
Syrup dispensers or pitchers	To distribute the paints

APPROPRIATE SURFACES

Clay, non-hardening, and water base	Oilcloth, back
	Papier-maché
Colored construction paper	Sawdust
Corrugated paper	Stone
Manila paper	Wood
Metal	X-ray film
Newsprint paper	Others

If powder paint is to be applied on an oily or slippery surface such as tin, glass, X-ray film, and non-hardening clay, for better adherence add cleansing powder or soap to the paint.

INTRODUCTION AND STORAGE OF BRUSHES

To acquaint young children with the tools of painting—brushes of various sizes and bristles, sponges, and others—encourage their use to apply water on the chalkboard. Young children might need to be shown how to hold their brush. The grip of a brush is similar to holding a spoon, with the fingers slightly straighter and more relaxed.

When ready, let the children work with paint on their brush. Sometimes other colors are discovered when more than one color is on their brush. Therefore, the children do not need to be extremely careful about cleaning their tools every time at first. However, a jar half-filled with water is desirable so that they can rinse their brushes whenever they want, as well as clean them when finished. Show the boys and girls how to roll the bristles of the round pointed brushes in the palm of their hand to form a point. Place them in the jar with the end of the handle on the bottom to protect the bristles from becoming bent and twisted. For summer storage, spray the bristles with a moth repellent.

MIXING THE PAINT

Regardless of the intended use of the paint, shake the dry powder paint and water together in a screw-top jar.

For *painting pictures,* a paint similar to a consistency of heavy white sauce is good. Young children seem to find thick paint easier to handle and to clean up. Before shaking the water and paint together, add wheat paste to thicken it. If the particular

What I Do to Keep Healthy—*John J., age five*

Observe a young child brushing his teeth; only then is the feeling expressed in this 24 x 36 inch painting fully understood. Intuitively John enlarged the important parts: the drippy toothbrush, the smeary mouth, and the triangular-shaped arms. Because legs are unimportant when he brushes his teeth, John symbolized them with two little stubs.

What I Enjoyed About the Circus—*Barbara W., age nine*

Barbara's use of bright colors and her carefully worked-out details express the atmosphere of the circus. The color and decoration on their car and their hats centers the interest on the clowns' performance.

Decoration—*Gail H., age seven*

Only her teacher was aware of Gail's remarkable motor control and interest span. She methodically detailed a few eggs each day for two weeks. Wisely, some of the eggs were left undecorated.

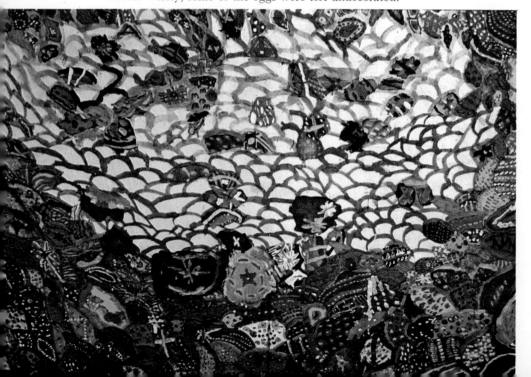

Something For
Our Drama-
tization—
  *Sondra M.,
  age nine*

A Toy For Another Child—*Patty N.,
  age eleven*

The bright red-orange stocking that forms the legs, arms, and faces contrasts dramatically with the black braids and the burlap dress. What an endearing interpretation! The self-selected topic conveys Patty's motherly nature. A message was tied around the doll's neck: "I'm a girl of 2. I had a lot of fun making this Indian doll and I hope you will like it. If you can will you please write to tell me about you. Your friend, Patty."

160C

My Favorite Part of the Christmas Story—*Cedric L., age eleven*

What the Music Reminds Me of (Strauss' "The Blue Danube Waltz")—
Janice L., age twelve

brand of powder paint flakes off the finished picture when dry, add cleansing powder next time. Mixing a little formaldehyde (A POISON) with the paint will help to keep it sweet.

If the fluidity of paint seems to bother the children, perhaps for a while a more static medium such as chalk, crayon, or cut paper would satisfy them more. For the beginner, two colors of paint are adequate; for example, a bright one and a dark one.

When children are ready to handle more colors, provide red, yellow, blue, black and white paint. With these basic colors, children sometimes mix colors as they work. A mixture of paints on the brush forms another color on the paper, for example:

blue + yellow = green	blue + red = violet
yellow + black = green	red + yellow + blue = gray
yellow + red = orange	to dull a color, add black or
orange + black or blue =	brown
brown	to lighten a color, add white

For *activities other than illustration,* a less thick paint consistency is desirable. Vary the proportion of the water to the paint. Test it on the material to be used. If it flows easily from the brush and if the material absorbs it well, the consistency is right. Most materials respond to powder paint that is similar to the consistency of medium white sauce.

If the powder paint cakes from dryness, soak it with water

How I Think I Look—

Lee Ann H., age five

Why did Lee Ann eliminate her shoulders? Perhaps from a five-year-old's view of herself, they are just a part of a dress. But Lee Ann certainly observed the decoration of her clothes —the necklace, the polka dots, and the anklets.

161

for several days. Lumps in the paint can be removed by straining it through nylon or a food strainer.

SUITABLE CLASSROOM PAINTING AREAS

When easel painting is first introduced, let as many children paint as possible. If easels are not available, place papers at appropriate working heights on the chalkboard and corkboard. However, the floor and the tables provide flat horizontal surfaces which many children prefer because they can move around or turn their painting as they work. One second grader volunteered the explanation, "I turn my paper so I can get at it."

Of course, not always will many children paint at once. Most frequently, a rotation plan is organized in which one or two children paint at the easel while others work with different art media or other areas of learning.

ORGANIZATION OF SUPPLIES

For *painting pictures,* if the chalkboard is used as an easel, place the half-filled paint jars on the chalk trays. Press non-hardening clay around the base of the jars to firmly secure them. At the easel, of course, keep the paints, container of brushes and jar of water in the easel tray ready for use. For the horizontally flat painting surfaces, designate the areas by opened newspapers with nearby supplies to share. Children can help organize the supplies. After the placement of the paint brushes and water, let the children tape their own papers on the upright surfaces at appropriate working heights.

If the *three-dimensional forms to be painted* require small amounts of paint, use a papier-maché egg carton or a muffin tin for a paint container to be shared by a few children. The pan can be cleaned easier if the muffin tin is greased or lined with paper cups. If more paint is needed, organize a paint table with the necessary supplies in the middle. Let a group of children work at the paint table until finished.

DRYING THE PAINTINGS

Because many powder paint illustrations are large, drying space is at a minimum. A clothes drying rack is handy for the paper supply as well as for drying. Some easels are equipped with a drying rack. Surfaces under tables also provide good drying areas. If the easel or chalkboard isn't used immediately, let the painting dry on the work surface.

PAINTING ON THREE-DIMENSIONAL FORMS

Some children prefer to paint directly on the object, whereas others, due to their concern about the appearance of the end product, want to plan their design. Powder paint is a good planning medium. Encourage these children to practice on everyday objects with surfaces similar to the final product; for example, mailing tubes, oatmeal, and gift boxes. Children then have the opportunity to develop skills necessary to paint on a curved or flat three-dimensional surface. Frequently, alterations occur when the final product is painted; however, usually the final design satisfies the child more than the practice one.

PAINT "PRINTING"

Children at some time have the desire to duplicate their work over and over again. An elementary yet challenging process is paint "printing."

Use a thought-stimulating question to encourage them to discover the items at home that are appropriate to print with. The individuals within a sixth grade class discovered many ways to print with their odds and ends. Vivian curled her jagged-edged inner tube, daubed it on the paint pad, and bounced it up and down on her paper. Her neighbor responded, "Oh, that looks itchy." Another child brushed paint on the rim of a half pan of watercolor to get an oval shape on her paper. Many types of already-manufactured forms were pushed, whirled, and wiggled back and forth in attempts to discover the possibilities.

This six-year-old expresses a personal delight in walking to school in the rain. The decorative umbrella does not seem to protect her!

What Happens
on a Rainy Day—

child, age six

Exploring With Paint Printing—*Gene K., age nine*

Nine-year-old Gene stamped a wet sponge of paint on her paper, thus dividing it into various-sized rectangles. Her colorful washes of yellow paint accentuate the already rectangular design. The darker wavy line contrasts to the many straight-edged shapes.

Likewise in a third grade class, the inventions quickened as the children better acquainted themselves with the process of paint "printing." Some combined various colors while others overlapped them very experimentally. The teacher's question, "Well, how did you do that?" brought a variety of thoughtful independent answers from the children.

. . . Janet explained, "I took this," she held up a square of corrugated paper, "and just blotted it down on the paper like this." Her paper revealed squares of parallel lines.

. . . Keith had a row of spiral shapes on his paper. He demonstrated, "I put paint on this curlique and stamped it on the paper like this." His printing tool was a pipe cleaner coil with a little upright stem for a handle.

. . . Proud of her achievement, Beth offered as she pushed a dangling strand of hair off her forehead, "I painted the edges of a box; then I went one way and then the other way. It looks like a star." Beth had repeatedly stamped the painted edge of her paper reinforcement box from a central point on her paper. To give variety to the wheel shapes, she later squeezed the box to give the radiating points a different effect.

. . . Having applied her paint to the side of a cone-shaped thread spool, Marie explained, "I rolled it up the paper and then dragged it for a little bit."

The following day, each child used his favorite discoveries to print a portfolio cover for some of his schoolwork.

9. SAWDUST

Suggested for children
ages five through twelve

- characteristics of sawdust

- recipes, class-sized

- basic supplies

- source and storage of the flour and sawdust

- preparation

- selection of a color

- introduction

- other forms made by children

- drying

- finishing

- re-using sawdust

166

CHARACTERISTICS OF SAWDUST

Little working mess accompanies sawdust. Because the particles dry quickly, sawdust is easily swept from the floor and rubbed off the children's hands. As one third grader concluded, "It's nice to clean up." Other children too have freely shared their ideas.

. . . Sixth grader Donna commented, "It's different, it dries out into something you can keep."

. . . A little seven-year-old added shyly, "It's such a nice look."

. . . Loren, a fourth grader, gleefully contributed, "It seems so complete without being painted."

. . . A kindergarten child said, "I handle it easier."

However, sawdust lacks the cohesiveness of clay. This presents a problem to the children who use the stick-on method of working. For them, provide toothpicks and pipe cleaners to insert through their individually modeled forms before they are assembled.

A CLASS-SIZED RECIPE

Takes thirty minutes. Makes 38 orange-sized balls.

Combine in a dishpan:

18 cups sawdust
16 cups flour
6 tablespoons salt

Divide batch in half if two colors are desired. Place in another dishpan.

Blend in 3 tablespoons of powder paint to each batch if solid colors are wanted. Leave one-half of batch uncolored, if desired.

Gradually add small amounts of boiling water. Blend thoroughly after each addition until the mixture resembles a stiff, flaky, adhesive dough. If it becomes sticky, add dry sawdust.

Sprinkle 3 tablespoons of powder paint over the batch if a marbelized effect is desired. Mix.

Shape into balls the size of an orange.

BASIC SUPPLIES

Newspaper	To protect desktops
Plastic bag	To store unused modeling sawdust
Powder paint, fabric, crayon, paper, and other miscellany	To clarify the details
Sawdust balls, one for each child	To model with
Table	To place the forms on to dry
Toothpicks, wire or pipe cleaners	To use for structural supports within the forms and for details
Wire mesh or oven grates	To elevate forms while drying to minimize mildew

SOURCE AND STORAGE OF THE FLOUR AND SAWDUST

If each child brings a cupful from home, there's enough flour for several sawdust experiences. Have the children pour their contribution into a large unused paste jar. To indicate the cup capacity, mark the side of the container with tape or nail polish so that it can serve the double purpose of measurement and storage. If flour from home is not feasible, the room or school treasuries can perhaps supply the funds to purchase it.

Sawdust is obtainable from a number of places. Home workshops, lumber yards, school shops and millwork manufacturers usually are pleased to get rid of their sawdust.

PREPARATION

A four or six member committee of children can prepare sawdust, but the classroom teacher's guidance is needed. The handling of the boiling water is safest if done by the teacher. One twinkling little third grader commented as she helped mix the flour and sawdust, "Uh-m-m, it feels like soft sand at the beach." After the boiling water was added, the children formed balls from handfuls of sawdust. Suddenly Lynn burst forth, "They feel so good, I want to eat them."

OTHER FORMS MADE BY CHILDREN
Animals:

As his contribution to the Zany Zoo, Kim, a second grader, made a seal complete with red pipe cleaners coiled for the eyes and the ball. All of these finishing touches were added while the sawdust was still wet.

What I'd Like For My Birthday—

Mary Ellen J., age eight

Mary Ellen squeezed and pulled the sawdust until the form satisfied her. By making the legs and ears thick, she built a strong form. The brown eyes and slightly upturned mouth add appeal to this chubby sawdust teddy bear.

Beads:

Fifth grader Sharon poked a needle through the middle of her bead forms. When they were dry, she painted each bead with a decorative design. After covering each one with clear brushing lacquer, Sharon strung them on a heavy cord to wear as a necklace.

People:

To illustrate the time she was most frightened, fourth grader Mary was governed by her emotions. She made herself a quad amputee with pipe cleaner braids jutting out from her head, enlarged red button eyes, and strands of yarn wrapped around her waist. Her written story clarified her feelings about it. ". . . My mother was bitten by a dog named Spot. I was so frightened my braids stood out straight. Now, I'm afraid to play with Spot because he might bite me." Perhaps she eliminated her limbs because of their susceptibility to dog bites.

Pictures:

With his sawdust horse that was flat on one side, Eugene, a sixth grader, wanted to make a picture for his room. Holding it securely, he sewed it onto sturdy cardboard. The colorful yarns were placed vertically so that in addition to

Experimenting With Sawdust—

Bill A., age nine

By inserting pipe cleaners into his wet sawdust basket, Bill made sturdy handles. He then painted the handles and basket to match.

169

The Time
I Was
Frightened—

Mary L., age nine

a clever method of fastening, they also formed a decorative, striped saddle.

Planters:

A sixth grader packed a cardboard box with sawdust. Then he scooped out the center. As a precaution against mold, he cut away the sides of the box. When it was dry, he lined the sawdust planter with a piece of metal foil to prevent the moisture from seeping through.

Puppet Heads:

Some fourth graders modeled the heads of their favorite storybook characters. Because some children worked with the sawdust flat on the desks, the heads were flat in back. Others were round from all views. After the features were determined, they concentrated on the size of the neck opening and provisions to attach the clothes. The necks needed to be large enough to slip loosely over a finger. Sawdust necks with holes poked around the bottom were some of the solutions. Others rolled a piece of cardboard to form a neck for their puppet head. The cardboard necks were inserted while the sawdust was still wet. A week later when the heads were dry, the puppet's clothing was easily attached. The diminutive torso of Sondra's clown contributed a gentle humor to her dramatic, ad-libbed adventures with him.

DRYING

So that the work of little children can be identified when dry, have them print their name on the paper on which their finished work stands. The time needed to dry the sawdust forms is dependent on their sizes. An orange-sized form usually takes a week to dry thoroughly. To minimize mold, turn the forms occasionally to expose all parts to the air, or elevate them on oven racks or wire mesh.

If cracks appear during the drying process, use wood filler or a sticky flour paste to fill them. The filled-in crack will not be noticeable if it is covered with paint or a fabric.

FINISHING

The color of the sawdust itself is attractive to some children. Therefore the forms do not need to be decorated with paint or crayons unless the child desires. Part of the form can be painted or colored and part of it left the color of the sawdust. The sawdust form can also be painted over completely with powder paint. Other materials such as paper or fabric can be added to clarify the details.

One boy used toothpicks for the teeth of his sawdust puppet. Another sprinkled dry sawdust on for his horse's mane. One child discovered he could paint his sawdust form while it was still wet.

Due to their short attention span, encourage the children to finish while their interest is at its height and the sawdust is still wet. When the forms are dry a week later, some little children do not recognize their work.

RE-USING SAWDUST

In a cool place such as a refrigerator, sawdust keeps for a week. However, a crust forms on top unless the sawdust is wrapped in a damp cloth, plastic, or aluminum foil.

10. THREAD

Suggested for children
ages eight through twelve

- basic supplies

- first experiences

- appropriate backgrounds

- looms

- needles

- stitches

- use of scraps

- ways of working

- finishing

- storage of thread

BASIC SUPPLIES

For Stitchery

Fabrics, different colors, sizes........To allow children a choice
and textures _____ of size, color, and texture

Chalk or crayon.................................To outline or fill in areas for
those who desire

Iron and ironing board................To press fabrics

Needle threader ....To thread needles for those
who can't succeed other-
wise

Needles, medium and large,........To fit the variation of
straight with long eyes _____ threads, t a p e s, ribbons,
Bodkins _____ and fabrics

Paper, want ad section..................To cut models for clothes
and containers, if desired

Scrap items such as buttons,........To supplement fabrics
threads, feathers, and others

Scissors ....To cut fabrics and threads

Threads of different weights and....To stitch with
colors

Towel or fabric, solid color,..........To wrap the work for stor-
preferably light dull green _____ age and to use on a child's
lap or desk for a restful
background for the eyes
while working

For Weaving:

Cardboard ....To make looms

Looms, child-made or commer-......To carry thin weft threads
cial; needles, metal or small _____ across the loom from side
wooden shuttles or bodkins _____ to side

Salvage cords, ribbons, string,......To supplement yarns
ropes, and others

Scissors ....To cut the yarns

Rulers and pencils ....To measure and mark off
points on the looms

Threads of various weights and....To form the up and down
colors _____ threads on the loom—the
warp—as well as horizon-
tal weft threads for the
filling

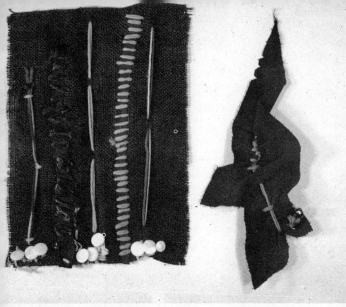

Experimenting
With Threads—

Amy M., age eight

Well supplied with miscellany from home, Amy worked with a needle and a bodkin on corduroy and burlap. Her two experiments reveal that she tested her materials in a variety of ways: Shirred and flat fabrics, long and short stitches, vertical and horizontal stitches, yarn and ribbon threads, and appliqué, topped off with a bell on one exploration and rows of buttons on the other.

FIRST EXPERIENCES

Children can analyze the needlework design and the woven structure of clothes. A fifth grade group observed some fabrics through a magnifying glass. Some commented about the qualities. "It kinda shows lines in different ways up and across." Jacqueline was impressed with the little holes. She said, "I could weave in and out of them to make a design." The study of fabrics from a foreign country, a family heirloom, a field trip to a museum or a textile plant, are other firsthand experiences that enhance children's desire to work with thread.

To stimulate further group thinking, question them. To illustrate: "What colors pleased you most?" "What materials did you enjoy touching?" "What materials could you bring from home?" "In what ways were the threads used?"

When children have stated certain opinions and questions about the fabrics, encourage them to hunt up some of their own materials. It is a real challenge.

APPROPRIATE BACKGROUNDS

For Stitchery

A fabric should be both durable and pliable. For picture backgrounds, the more porous materials such as burlap, open mesh vegetable sacks, or dishcloths promote success. However, it's surprising how some capably manipulate even very delicately structured fabrics. For example, a fourth grader explained as she worked with cheesecloth, "I pulled out three threads, some broke, but I picked them out with a needle. Now I will run a colored yarn through part of it."

To sensitize youngsters to the importance of appropriate fabric selection, discuss the fabric in relation to its use. For example, the texture of sheeting is suitable for puppet clothes and containers, whereas monk's cloth is appropriate for picture backgrounds and some containers. The following materials have been successfully used by children:

Burlap	Monk's cloth
Corduroy	Net
Dishcloth	Sacking for vegetables and fruits
Felt	Sheeting
Gauze	Toweling

For Weaving

The background is usually a series of lengthwise parallel threads (warp) through which crosswise threads are interlaced over and under. The threads used for warp vary from thick candlewicking to thin carpet warp. The type of warp is dependent on the purpose of the finished product as well as the eye and muscular coordination of the child.

What I Like to Do—

Jeanne E., age eight

In Jeanne's second experience with thread, she expressed her fondness for kites. After prominently stitching an interpretation of herself with her kite in front of the ground line, she completed it with conspicuously placed intials. The burlap fringe that surrounds the wooden frame adds distinction.

My Favorite Character—*Jay R., age eight*

Deeply interested in pioneer clothes, Jay created his own version of an American frontiersman. He snipped shapes from felt and suede for some of the colorful, characteristic details. The oval embroidery hoop not only kept his work flat but it also framed his favorite character.

LOOMS

Commercial looms of metal, plastic, and wood have been used successfully by children. Self-made cardboard ones are good too. Cardboard looms can be square, irregular in shape, triangular, circular, and rectangular. Some children gain real satisfaction through loom construction because they can then determine the shape and size of the loom. To provide for shrinkage of the woven fabric, make the loom wider and longer than the desired size of the weaving. Some of the possibilities for looms are:

An old picture frame

Wooden rulers

Wooden boards nailed together

Wooden box

Dowel rods inserted into wooden discs

Flat pieces of cardboard or cardboard boxes

Regardless of the material used for a square or rectangular loom, measure equidistant points at about ¼ inch from the edge on the opposite short sides. The manual dexterity of the child should determine the distance between the warp threads. Less mature children can better succeed with broader spaces. At these points, cut notches or slits, or securely pound in nails slightly angled toward the middle of the loom. At each lengthwise side of the loom, punch holes or pound nails on which the warp threads can be fastened at the beginning and the end.

Pull the warp thread through the hole or around the nail. Fasten securely with a knot. Bring this warp thread up the loom to the first notch or nail and across to the opposite notch or nail on the other edge, put it under to the second notch or nail, and then back across the loom to the second notch or nail. Repeat this until the loom is strung with threads parallel with the sides. Tie the thread securely to the punched hole or the nail on the opposite side of the loom.

For a two-sided form such as a rectangular or square purse, string the cardboard loom with an equal number of warp threads on both sides. When the weft thread completes the first side, turn the loom over to weave on the back side. When finished, the open sides will need to be fastened together somehow. For a purse with closed sides, carry the weft thread around from one side of the loom to the other; thus, both front and back are woven at the same time.

After the fourth graders independently solved the method of attaching the warp to the loom, Russell's arrangement was distinctive. He inserted an equal number of cardboard pegs into the two opposite sides of his rectangular cardboard loom. Proud to explain it to interested classmates, Russell said, "I used my scissors for the holes. Then I put in little chunks of cardboard. I put the string around them. When I get done weaving, then I'll pull the cardboard pieces out." Recognition of his original achievement helped to persuade Russell that his work could be

Exploring With Weaving—

Conrad H., age eleven

Coupled with gay colors were varied materials of interest. Rope left over from the paper sale formed the warp threads, while cotton, felt, and raffia intermingled for the filling. Vivid orange raffia stitched over the edges gives a refreshing irregularity.

177

significant. Previously, he was noted for his repertoire of annoyances.

NEEDLES

Sturdy needles are easily grasped by most children ages eight through twelve. The thickness of the thread determines the size and type of needle. For most stitchery activities, the manufactured metal needles with long eyes are essential. At times some children find it difficult to thread yarn. Sharing their method with perplexed classmates, two six-grade girls explained, "I twisted it on the end and then got it to a point." The other child added, "I licked the end of the yarn and flattened it with my fingers. Then it was easy to thread." It's also helpful to fold the yarn tautly over the needle and then push it through the eye. The fold keeps the yarn from splitting into numerous strands. Another method is to wrap a tiny piece of cellulose tape around the tip of the yarn. The tape then slips easily through the eye and is cut off after the needle is threaded. If a child still has difficulty, provide a needle threader—preferably the commercial type—or, as a last resort, a willing and able classmate.

Weaving needles and shuttles can be made from cardboard, bobby pins, wood scraps, wire, or tongue depressors. To carry the thread, cut a long opening into the material, if necessary. If thick yards are used for the weft, needles aren't needed. They can be put in by hand.

STITCHES

Children develop skill in the manipulation of stitches. To involve them in more than the mechanics of the medium, stimulate their thoughts and feelings first so that they can translate them into form.

Initial experiences usually result in some "refreshingly different" attempts. When the desire to know more stitches increases, children can teach each other or use needlework books as resources. But keep in mind the importance of developing the child's abilities to express himself genuinely. Each child can "invent" stitches to meet his own needs.

USE OF SCRAPS

For Stitchery

When children have the urge to *stitch pictures,* question them. "What could you bring from home that can somehow be sewn onto cloth?" Children usually think of common sewable items as well as the unusual; for example, binding tape, buckles, ribbons, corks, soda straws, rick-rack, buttons, fabric scraps, sponges, mirrors, toothpicks, laces, wire mesh, and pipe cleaners. From an active search at home, many scraps of interest from the family ragbag are uncovered.

When the array of salvage materials arrive, bring out the children's ideas in a group discussion. "What part of a person is as round as this button?" "What do you have at your desk to finish that picture?" "What does the design of this wire mesh remind you of?" "Who else might be in this picture?" "What could be used to represent the man's hair?" "What do you think of when you see this color?" "How could it become a humorous picture?"

Through questioning, personal responses and original ideas are aroused. Sometimes the color, the feel, and the shape of the scrap stimulate the development of delightful portrayals. When asked how their pictures started, some little eight-year-olds gave the following answers:

. . . "I found a scrap that looked like a rocket car."

. . . "The little curls in it [braid] reminded me of a rug."

. . . "This blue blanket reminded me of water. I'm going to make a boat with an anchor, oar, and some people. Then maybe a sun."

. . . "The color and the wool reminded me of a tree with beads for apples."

. . . "It's a kitten. It's velvet, too!"

. . . "These [pine cones] reminded me of a train."

. . . "It's a fairy rainbow of velvet, and red hair ribbon."

With the touch of a child's ingenuity, discards are transformed into genuine personal statements. With emphasis placed on the children's ideas, they boldly discover their own methods to sew a picture, a puppet, a container, or whatever they desire.

For Weaving

Encourage the children to investigate their own community resources to discover weaving materials. Many children view indigenous materials with new appreciation when they have woven with them. A broad selection insures a more enriched and individual experience. The following materials have been creatively used in weaving:

Bamboo	Jute	Tinsel
Cellophane	Oilcloth	Willow
Confetti wire	Pine needles	Yarn
Cork strips	Plastic strips	Others
Corn husks	Raffia	
Grasses	Reeds	

WAYS OF WORKING

For Stitchery

Some children cut the separate parts and then sew them together. For instance, tree branches are cut separate from the trunk, and then placed in slightly overlapped positions on the trunk. Some fasten them down to the picture's background unconcerned about the raw edges. One sixth grade perfectionist, Larry, worked differently. With chalk he carefully outlined the entire shirt and then turned the raw edges under. Methodically he sewed it to the background with running stitches. He understood the success quotient involved in mature planning.

Dalton, an inquisitive nine-year-old, playfully folded and refolded some brown corduroy. Accidentally, the lapped over end formed the head of a fish. He fastened it to the background with a big button that symbolized the eye.

Containers and puppet clothes also stimulate various ways of

Something I'd Like To Own—

Floyd I., age nine

On a rectangular loom, Floyd produced a handsome marble bag. After he sewed the side seams together, he made a drawstring for the top.

working. Some devise structural designs that require fewer seams, whereas others are more complex. Fifth grader Winifred told about her method of cutting a cloth puppet. "I folded the cloth double, took the scissors, and then cut the shape." Basting the two pieces together, she used fabric shapes to indicate the details of the all-in-one-piece puppet.

Loren, another original thinker, folded one side of the fabric over the paint box and two pencils as they laid on some green fabric. He explained, "I'm going to make a cover for my paints and pencils. I'm glad the cloth is big enough for it. Then I can make a yarn handle so I can carry them home."

Develop a sensitivity to the uniqueness of something in a child's work. Perhaps it's not new to you, but it might be a revelation to the child. Admire the content of the picture, a novel way of working, or a unique use of a material.

. . . Sixth grade Gerald crayoned dots as guides for his needle.

. . . An eleven-year-old outlined the sails of his boat with three light-colored yarns. At regular intervals with a single yarn, he stitched it down at right angles.

. . . Sandra, a third grader, incorporated her initials, S.S., under one window of her building.

. . . For a backing for his picture, twelve-year-old Hans stapled his fringed stitchery onto a stiff cardboard. To make it useable, he placed a gummed picture hanger on the back.

. . . Marcia used the vertical stripes of the puppet's dress as guide lines for some simple stitches.

. . . A shiny belt buckle to represent the grill was stitched down for Walt's toy jalopy.

. . . To symbolize the shape of her head, a third grader used a transparent marble. Her picture included her surroundings when she was in bed with the measles.

. . . Cleverly, a fourth grader represented the handle of the lawn mower with rick-rack and the wheels with shiny silver buttons.

. . . Eleven-year-old Ann discovered that heavy yarns often "pinch" lightweight fabrics. Next time she's going to use thinner threads and flatten her work as she sews.

181

What I Imagined in My Scraps—*Suzanne H., age twelve*

At top level of enthusiasm, Suzanne created button-head Donald on a tricycle. Liking her own blend of scraps, the picture became Daddy's gift on Father's Day. The written composition that followed added meaning to her work: ". . . Donald lived with his father, who was a college professor of botany, and mother, in a cottage in Puerto Rico. It was near Father's Day and Donald was worried about what he would get his father. He thought, 'I will go and see my two friends Kim and Kammy. . . .' They walked half way up the hill and there they found several beautiful rare flowers. They came home, Donald pulling the wagon and his pals behind him. . . . Donald gave his father the beautiful rare flowers. . . . Donald was so happy; his little brown-faced friends enjoyed making Donald's father happy too."

For Weaving

Most children prefer to vary their weaving count; weaving over three warp threads and under two might be changed and repeated later on the same piece of weaving. Improvised and alternated thread counts add interest to the weft. Some children have been observed to change count naturally with a different color or texture.

FINISHING

For Stitchery

A few children may not have the attention span necessary to complete their ideas. Perhaps the medium causes eye fatigue. Make allowances for these differences among children.

Stitches can be supplemented with crayon. Some fabrics can even be glued or inconspicuously stapled to the background.

All work is improved by pressing. Place a slightly dampened cloth on the back side and press. If an ironing board isn't available, protect a table surface with the kind of paper insulated bags that sometimes enclose new books or ice cream.

If the stitchery is a picture, tape all four sides onto a sturdy material, such as chipboard. If desired, a mat can surround it. For a large wall hanging, sew several plastic or metal hanger loops in a horizontal row on the top back. To help it hang evenly, insert a dowel rod within the loops. A metal rod hung at the bottom helps to keep it taut.

For Weaving

When the weaving is finished, bend the cardboard loom slightly and lift to release the warp threads from their places. With a wooden loom, lift the individual warp threads off from the slightly angled nails. Cut the knots on the warp ends, bring them around the first weft thread and tuck them parallel to the outside warp threads. If there are any loose ends on the underside, tuck them in with the weft of the same color.

STORAGE OF THREAD

For quick selection, store wool yarns in a glass or plastic container. Ribbons and other types of thread can be wound around mailing tubes or strips of cardboard with U-shaped notches on the sides. Fasten the thread ends with snips of cellulose tape or common pins.

183

11. WATERCOLOR

Suggested for children

ages nine through twelve

- form of purchase

- basic supplies

- use of paints and brushes

- appropriate backgrounds

- first experiences

- other media on watercolor backgrounds

- techniques developed while working

184

BASIC SUPPLIES

Brushes, large and small, soft and stiff, round and flat — To discover the possibilities of a variety of brushes

Charcoal or chalk — To outline shapes, if a child outlines first

Coffee pot, pitcher or No. 2 coffee can — To pour water into individual containers

Jars, or food cans, shallow but good sized — To hold ample water at individual desks so that changing and refilling water becomes unnecessary.

Oilcloth or plastic — To provide a smooth surface and to protect the desk

Paper, manila, 9 x 12 inch and 12 x 18 inch — To provide a choice in the size of paper

Rags, large clean white or sponges — To wipe off excess water and paint from the brushes, paper and box

Refills, paint, and brush — To refill cakes of color and replace brushes

Water — To make the paint cakes fluid, to dampen paper and brushes, and to clean the brushes while working

Watercolors, in tubes of basic colors or one eight-color box for each child — To provide each child with a choice of colors to paint with

FORM OF PURCHASE

Watercolor is available through most supply houses in two forms—the dry and semi-moist cakes and the liquid in tubes. The liquid paint permits quick application. Due to elementary school children's short interest span, liquid watercolor paints have an advantage. Perhaps because they are less expensive, the dry and semi-moist cake forms are popular. The boxes with eight colors and a brush are preferable to boxes with more colors. The limited number of colors challenge children to mix other colors of their own. To facilitate use, it's important to soften the cakes with water.

USE OF PAINTS AND BRUSHES

As children work from one cake of color to another, naturally color remnants are left on the paint. The mixture affects the intensity of the colors. Often subtle colors result. When finished, those children who prefer the pure, bright colors, automatically wipe off each cake of color; others leave some remnants on the paint or cakes purposely. Up to a certain extent, an intermingling of a few colors doesn't affect watercolor experiences.

Discuss the use and structure of the paintbrush; for example, the brush needs to be wet before it is stroked over the paint. However, if a brush is left in water, the glue softens and soon the bristles drop out. At the end of the art experience, clean the brush with water and roll round, pointed bristles in the palm to bring them to a point. Store the brushes either with the handle end down in a jar, or in flat position in the paint box.

APPROPRIATE BACKGROUNDS

Colored construction paper, sandpaper, watercolor paper, and the newspaper want-ad section are good surfaces. Children in a combination fifth and sixth grade shared their ideas about the use of the want-ad section for a paint surface. "I don't like it 'cause you can see the writing." . . . "This paper ain't so bad; the colors soak through." . . . "I like it. The paint dries a little faster. You don't get paint all over." Have an assortment of papers available to enable children to discover what they like to use. Then when choices are given, they'll have reasons for their selection.

> Patty freely painted yellow-orange and blue lines on her 12 x 18 inch paper. Suddenly she noticed a shape that resembled a bird. With a darker color, Patty outlined the bird shape and added other details. Patty's original bird has a personality often lost when children set out to draw one.

Getting Ideas As I Work—

Patty S., age nine

What I Liked About Alaska—

Marianne W., age nine

Familiarity with watercolor had developed skills to use it with confident control. With her "frosted," lyrical igloos and mountains, Marianne created a feeling of the warm yet friendly, sturdy people.

FIRST EXPERIENCES

With a new medium, older children are sometimes hesitant until they have succeeded in pleasing themselves and their classmates. Let the children explore its possibilities. Paint on dry paper; then, for comparison, sprinkle water on another piece. With a brush, flip the paint on the wet paper. Tilt it to watch the paint flow. Experiment with a semi-dry stiff-bristled brush on wet and dry papers. Of course, in such a fluid medium many accidents happen. Children need time to discover not only the

Gary brushed the entire paper with clear water. Then he touched his color-loaded brush to the dampened paper. His colors blending together formed irregular shapes that reminded him of an aquarium. With black paint Gary interpreted the forms of the fish and underwater growth.

Getting Ideas
From Paint
Splashes on
Wet Paper—

*Gary G.,
age ten*

How I'd Like to Look For a Masquerade—

Richard G., age twelve

Rapidly painting on wet paper, Richard distributed his colors intuitively. Suggesting only a few of the clown's features, the picture gives the observer a chance to complete the clown in his own way.

blending of colors, but also methods to prevent watercolors from running together. Through experimentation, they become acquainted with the numerous possibilities of watercolor.

OTHER MEDIA ON WATERCOLOR BACKGROUNDS

Some children are less fearful of making a mistake when they work on a dry already-painted background. Encourage them to use their experiments as backgrounds for media in which they feel more competent: cut paper, crayon, paper sculpture, powder paint, and others. For example, cut paper or paper sculpture forms can be pasted onto the watercolor background to illustrate any general topic of meaning to the children.

The colors and the shapes of a dry background also stimulate the children to think of ideas. Backgrounds have suggested the different moods in the sky . . . sunsets or storms. To silhouette their objects against the sky, children can superimpose contrasting colors with either crayon, powder paint, or watercolor. Others who thought their background resembled an aquarium, added fish, rocks, and other objects to complete their idea.

However, give the children an opportunity to use plain sheets of paper, too. Some prefer them. The color of the paper itself often adds sparkle to the finished painting.

TECHNIQUES DEVELOPED WHILE WORKING

Children will discover various ways of handling watercolor as they work. For example, one boy discovered that a full wet brush

Something From Our Amazon River Trip—

Kathy C. and Louise, ages twelve

Helping to create a diorama, Louise painted the bottom of a cardboard box blue to represent the sky. Kathy cut foliage from oaktag. Together they taped the woods scene in the box. The lush foliage and the almond-studded tree trunks form an impressive jungle background for the playful monkeys and the birds.

of paint was necessary in order to paint a solid color. Some children have used a partially dry brush and barely touched the surface of their paper, thus achieving an effect of bark on a tree. A boy separated the bristles of his brush into two sections to create a striped effect on his paper.

Several colors can be on the brush at one time; for instance, one color on the tip of the brush, and other colors on the side of the brush. Sometimes a color is achieved accidentally when children work from one cake to another. Frequently children paint one color into another wet one, and a blending of the two occurs.

189

A classroom provides a pleasant setting for happy living and learning. As far as the situation permits, adjustments are aimed to attain a learning environment that is healthy, comfortable, and attractive.

The arrangement within a classroom can possess a friendly appearance of groomed spaciousness. What are the necessary ingredients? They might be: *organization, good housekeeping,* and an *awareness of the needs* of special age groups within the specific room.

FLOOR UTILIZATION

PROVIDE FREE, UNCLUTTERED FLOOR AREAS AROUND THE ENTRY.

This is not only more inviting, but it is also conducive to smooth and safe traffic flow.

COLOR SELECTION

KEEP FURNITURE DULL AND LIGHT IN COLOR.

This promotes more visual comfort; the furniture takes its place in the background.

PROVIDE A DOMINANT WALL COLOR.

This establishes an impression of spacious unity. Calmness is assisted through the use of inconspicuous grayed colors or neutrals. The choice of the color is determined by the room size, the number of windows, and the direction of the light. To illustrate: In a medium-sized classroom with windows all along the north wall, use a light value to make the room seem larger. Because a north exposure receives no direct sunlight, warm, grayed colors, such as yellow and yellow green, add cheerfulness to the room.

PROVIDE A *FEW* PLANTS WITH LARGE, INTERESTING FOLIAGE IN CONTAINERS WITH SUBDUED COLOR AND SIMPLE FORM.

This provides learning experiences in the care of plants. It also contributes a feeling of warmth to the room. An unobtrusive container emphasizes the plant.

FURNITURE ARRANGEMENT

GROUP FURNITURE OF SIMILAR HEIGHT AND PURPOSE, PARALLEL TO THE WALL, IN SQUARE, RECTANGULAR, F, H, T, L, U OR E SHAPES.

This utilizes the space well, since it provides unoccupied floor area for safe living, individual pupil guidance, and activities. For example: The superiority of the after arrangement of the thirty-eight desks is obvious. The organization of the desks into different-sized and different-shaped areas utilizes the space more functionally. Two large L-shapes contrast with a small U-shaped group of desks. Even the spaciousness around the library table makes it very usable.

GROUP DESKS INTO SMALL FLEXIBLE UNITS THAT ALLOW CHILDREN TO FACE THE INSIDE WALLS.

This is considerate of the child's liking of small groups, his changing needs, and his need to protect his eyes from glare.

GROUP DESKS SO THAT CHILDREN SEE MORE FACES THAN BACKS.

This creates a friendly and functional arrangement. Reserve favorable locations for children with visual and audial difficulties.

PLACE THE TEACHER'S DESK INCONSPICUOUSLY TOWARD THE SIDE OF THE ROOM.

This allows for more informal observation and inconspicuous individual conferences.

ESTABLISH COMFORTABLY SPACIOUS CENTERS OF ACTIVITY TO BE USED BY CHILDREN FOR MULTIPURPOSES, IF NECESSARY.

This encourages independent work within a given space and supplements the work surfaces of the children's desks.

Before Arrangement of
Physical Properties
Third Grade

After Arrangement of
Physical Properties
Third Grade

MISCELLANEOUS

PROVIDE SOME EMPTY WALL SURFACES AND THE WINDOW WALL FOR EYE-REST SPACE.

An empty window wall preserves children's eyesight because their attention centers on inside walls. Uncluttered surfaces also contribute to restfulness, good work habits, and better living.

GROUP CHARTS TOGETHER.

This makes them not only more accessible to children, but it also provides a more orderly and artistic classroom. To protect charts from soil, store them in an inconspicuous place.

REMOVE GLASS FROM A PICTURE IF IT MIRRORS ROOM FURNISHINGS.

This makes it possible for all children to see the picture. For some protection, the reproduction can be waxed on the back side with transparent paste wax. If a more protective, non-glossy surface is desired, a commercial picture framer can heat press it to a sturdy cardboard and then spray it. Also available is a non-glare glass.

From time to time, evaluate the arrangement of the physical properties with the boys and girls. Seek out the children's ideas. "What places seem crowded? How could it be improved? How will it look? Let's try it." When children help to plan and to rearrange the furniture to meet their changing requirements, they are sensitized to beautiful and consistent furniture arrangement. At their level of understanding, provide opportunities for them to come in touch with a life-long challenge.

Getting Ideas From My Painted
Background—*Tom E., age twelve*

The dark-stained trail left by
some surplus water reminded
Tom of smoke rising from a chimney. With white powder paint
and watercolors, Tom completed
his idea. The subtly blended
colors in the white and yellow-
flecked sky convey the spirit of
a snowy winter day.

What I Would Like to Hunt—
Robert P., age twelve

The feathery sky colors contrast
sharply with the precisely painted
grass and bird in the foreground.
Robert's wish to do a realistic drawing of the bird is characteristic of
this age level.

Display Board on Candle Making

DISPLAY AREAS—TWO-DIMENSIONAL

The personal touch of the classroom is supplied by the teacher, the children, and their classroom experiences. Usually each classroom has a display board on which every child should frequently have his work. To the child, the display of his work enhances its value and demonstrates teacher acceptance. The arrangement of the board provides an opportunity to activate the children's powers to select and arrange discriminately. Now and then you arrange it. At other times, the display board is the children's responsibility.

An attractive display not only adds vitality to the general appearance of the classrooms, but it also gives an opportunity to communicate a message. Sometimes, its theme concerns daily discussions, while at other times it stimulates or culminates an activity. With the purpose for its use in mind, the following guides give direction to the artistic powers within you as well as the children.

If a display board is unavailable, use a discarded picture frame to enclose an inexpensive and sturdy display surface. With the

Display Board
on Month
of May—

*Mrs Myrtle
H. Rue,
second and third
grade teacher*

glass picture and cardboard removed, insert from the back a piece of tight-fitting insulation or corkboard. If the frame is to be refinished, paint it either to match the wall on which it is to be hung or the color of the cork or insulation board. Two or three frames grouped together provide useful display surfaces.

SELECTING THE MATERIALS

Guides

Suggested Applications

EXHIBIT *SOME CURRENT* CLASSROOM ACTIVITY ON THE EYE LEVEL OF THE CHILDREN.

This allows the children to see it and to arrange it within their own physical sphere of living. At the same time, it provides clues to the uniqueness of a particular group.

Because the function and space of the classroom limits the area for display, use one or two of the strong current interests. Shelve other interests in accessible yet inconspicuous places — book shelves, cupboards, chart files, and file drawers.

CHOOSE ITEMS THAT CAN BE SEEN WELL.

This invites the attention of children and guests to its message from many parts of the classroom.

Large items with contrasting values that can be viewed from a reasonable distance are appropriate; for example, pictures, posters, mobiles, plants, and others. For close observation and study, place small items such as newspaper clippings into attractive portfolios.

SELECT THE WORK OF DIFFERENT CHILDREN ON DIFFERENT DEVELOP-MENTAL LEVELS.

This is not only considerate of every child's feelings and rights, but it also shows a friendly appreciation of each individual's, work.

Even if space were available, it wouldn't be desirable to display every child's work. More significance is attached when the work reflects the child's best. So that each child is given equal and frequent opportunity, keep a checklist as a record.

SELECT BOTH TWO AND THREE - DIMENSIONAL MATERIALS.

This provides extra visual and tactile appeal. Use materials that are suitable to the theme or to the media to be displayed.

To add more tactile variety to a display of powder paintings, for instance, exhibit the basic tools such as the paint brushes and the cans of paint. For other displays, different items might be fitting. Dowel rods inserted into cork squares and a rolled fabric add tactile and visual appeal to the display of the children's Sunday activities.

USE SOFT COLORS OR NEUTRALS THAT ARE SLIGHTLY DARKER THAN THE LIGHTEST VALUE IN THE PICTURES FOR FRAMES, MOUNTS, AND BACKGROUNDS.

This focuses attention on the exhibited items. One color should be predominant, while others contrast in value and intensity.

Construction and corrugated paper offer numerous possibilities for frames that can be used repeatedly. For example:

Cut the paper the same height as the illustration but wider to allow the paper to be rolled toward the center on each side.

Use a tape hinge to attach the picture.

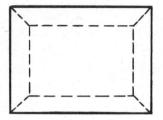

Cut the paper wider than the picture on all four sides. The width of the frame or mount increases when the picture has large objects or a great deal of movement. Then diagonally fold each one of the four corners. Bend the equal-sized margins over the picture. As shown in the diagram, the paper is folded forward on the dotted lines. Mount the picture from the front.

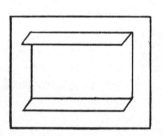

Cut all four sides of the paper wider than the picture. With a razor blade slit it in the shape of a broad capital H. Fold the upper and lower flaps to coincide with the height of the picture. Snip the flaps to the desired depth. Tape the picture onto the back.

Other items that can be used for frames are:
- transparent plastic berry boxes
- tops and bottoms of cardboard boxes
- paper fruit and vegetable trays

Mounts can be made from such materials as wire screen, gauze or burlap stretched over cardboard, colored paper, desk blotters, corrugated paper, and felt.

DISPLAY AREAS—THREE-DIMENSIONAL

In addition to the display board, exhibits can assume a number of forms.

TABLE DISPLAYS

Most often consist of three-dimensional work. By grouping materials that seem to belong together, interest and simplicity are gained. When height is desired, use wooden blocks or boxes to elevate some of the work. Cover the "commercial" on the box with paper, fabric, or paint.

One group of children displayed animals they were "most afraid of" on a sand table. With favorite stones from hobby collections, the children built a natural-looking cave amid deep foliage. They grouped their clay animals around the hollow of the cave—some going into it, one sleeping outside, and others on top. Similar arrangements can be made to illustrate other topics, such as "Our Visit to the Farm," or "What We Learned About Our Own State," or "Where I Would Like to Explore."

Some sixth graders revealed in papier-maché their winter interests—skating, making angels in the snow, running, walking with a dog, and even watching television indoors. For a background setting, they painted a long, narrow picture. To make the picture stand, wooden blocks were vertically glued onto the back.

GROUP AND INDIVIDUAL DISPLAY BOOKS

Vary in content according to the purpose. For example, pictures can be made to tell a story. For an individual's book, start with a self-portrait on the first page. From then on, pictures can reveal the child's personal response to general topics such as "What I'd Like to Be," "Using My Favorite Color," and "Something I'd Like to Own." Parents as well as children enjoy display books. A pictorial record of the child's growth and development over a certain span of time is another use of the book form. Periodically add some of the child's pictures.

A class of first graders made several group display books about their neighborhood helpers. Each group chose to illustrate a helper. The pictures were pasted on ruled paper with appropriate captions printed underneath, e.g., "Mother makes clothes for us," "She helps us get well when we are sick," and "Mother plans picnics for us." Ten illustrations, one from each member of the committee, were included to portray "Mother." The crayoned cover was made from sturdy brown wrapping paper to preserve it so that others, too, could enjoy it. Staples held the book together.

At times, cardboard gift boxes and correspondence portfolios are appropriate to file the children's work. The portfolios are made from sturdy paper with two half pockets inside. With a title on the front, the box or portfolio becomes an inviting display book with removable contents.

"MOVIE" OR "TELEVISION" SHOW BOXES

Appeal especially to young children. They are not only delighted when their own picture appears in the opening of the box, but it also encourages them to supply the verbal commentary.

To make the "movie film," paste the children's pictures next to one another on a roll of wrapping paper. For the cabinet, make an opening in the side of a cardboard box about the size of the children's pictures. If an orange crate is used, rip the cover off. Insert two dowel rods through holes in the top and bottom of the box for the turning mechanism. Tack the ends of the picture roll onto the two rods. And then everything is ready to show each piece of work.

Because today's classroom, so to speak, extends beyond the four walls, other display possibilities exist. After satisfying everyone's wishes with the classroom display, exhibit some child art in other areas of the school building. The principal, the custodian, and other school helpers are usually willing to have some in their offices. Walls of the gym, corridor, and the all-purpose room are other good areas. When the weather permits, or in southern climates, exhibit outdoors on the playground's fence or on a clothesline securely looped around tree trunks or stakes. And even the neighborhood baker and shoemaker are happy to be remembered with a display of art work by boys and girls who live within the community.

SUMMING UP

As an educator, you undoubtedly wonder whether you effectively guide the children in their art activities. As one way to find out, you evaluate your practices. Self-appraisal promotes desirable changes. It also reinforces strength, and stimulates a healthy awareness, as well as the hows and whys, of your growth.

A checklist will often serve to direct your attention to your teaching effectiveness. Look first at the *children* you are helping to develop.

Do the Children:

.... respond enthusiastically to the discussions and materials?

.... express experiences that are personal and unique?

.... work with self-confidence and growing discrimination?

.... appear to gain satisfaction from their work?

.... seem more aware of their environment?

.... assume responsibility for materials?

.... seem eager to pursue unfamiliar as well as familiar art media?

.... respect and accept the ideas, feelings, and understandings expressed by others as well as themselves?

To help you reach a conclusion about your arrangement of the classroom's *physical properties*, make use of the following questions.

Does the Classroom:

.... reveal an arrangement that suits the activity and the size of the group?

.... reflect a feeling of visual comfort through color and furniture arrangement?

.... convey a feeling of friendliness?

.... provide confortable activity areas to supplement the individual desks?

.... protect the children's eyesight?

.... reveal effective displays on the children's eye level?

Use your answers to these questions to help you evaluate whether you create a *permissive atmosphere:*

Do You:

.... believe all children have a desire to express themselves through art?

.... have faith in all children's powers of expression?

.... show enthusiasm, warm acceptance, and interest through your personal manner?

.... promote a warm friendliness among all children?

.... accept the purposeful noise and supply mix-up that accompany the manipulation of art materials?

.... respect each child's contributions and efforts?

The following list will help you gauge the quality of your *stimulation.*

Do You:

.... use thought-provoking questions that progress from the general to the more specific?

.... consider the weather, the time, the topic, and the attention span of the children?

.... spend sufficient time to insure enthusiastic individual responses?

.... use broad general topics based on children's actual, imaginative, and vicarious experiences?

.... use art media that are appropriate to the developmental levels of the children?

Your answers to the accompanying questions will help you make an inventory of your *guidance*.

Do You:

.... encourage all children to enjoy their art experiences?

.... provide opportunities for the children to select suitable sizes and colors from the available materials, the *specific* topic and sometimes the medium?

.... plan the distribution of art materials to avoid confusion and waste of time?

.... encourage children to combine media when it helps them to express their ideas and feelings?

.... allow children to work directly with the medium intended for the final product?

.... let the children work in a variety of positions?

.... praise some little unique discovery, habit, or artistic achievement?

.... encourage children to develop their own techniques?

.... develop the children's confidence in their ability to handle an unfamiliar medium?

.... provide successive experiences in all art media appropriate to the children's levels of development?

.... question a child wisely and gently to help him clarify his thinking?

.... when necessary, redirect the child's energies into problems that the child is able to solve?

.... reiterate the importance of safe and proper handling of tools?

.... permit children to finish their work while their interest and enthusiasm are at their height?

Answer the following questions to help you see whether *acceptance* plays a part in your methods of working with children.

Do You:

.... accept all children's interpretations of the general topic?

.... accept different ideas, feelings, and concerns of children as revealed through their visual and verbal interpretations?

.... show your enthusiasm for the children's world through your questions and comments, and through the frequent use of their work for classroom displays?

.... accept the child's way of working?

.... reveal flexibility in your responses?

.... recognize the existence of different degrees of development in the visual arts?

The following checklist will help you know how sensitive you are to children's *development levels.*

Do You Recognize:

.... that there are variances in maturity and personality within a group of children?

.... that all children's art work starts with the scribble and moves through the symbolic stage to more realistic portrayal?

.... that children relate color and details to the object as they mature?

.... that children's maturity determines their needs, appropriate topics, and media?

.... that occasionally children like to participate in a group endeavor?

.... that growth occurs at an uneven rate?

To appraise your methods of *evaluation,* use the following self-inventory.

Do You:

.... let the children set standards for individual and group achievement?

.... evaluate in a constructive manner?

.... evaluate the art experience and the art product on the basis of the child's behavior, his growth and development, his way of working, and the ideas and feelings he conveys through his work?

.... evaluate individually when needed during the work period as well as with the group at the conclusion of some experiences?

.... gather the children together to help them informally discuss, understand and respect the uniqueness of their individual interpretations?

.... save systematically some of the work as a record of each child's growth?

.... use evaluation as a summation of specific learnings, methods of working, and reactions to media?

.... use evaluation occasionally to link the present achievement to the next experience?

In addition, seek art experiences to help yourself grow in a creative way. Be aware, open-minded, enthusiastic, and explorative. Actively involve yourself in some art media, read about the creative experiences of others, visit art museums, and support the visual arts in your school and community. When you participate in a special way, you're better equipped to inspire children to enjoy and value creative individuality.

INDEX